Thank You

Aaron Hernandez, Aaron Vasquez, Aristotle Athiras, Aunt Kathy, Bindu Heck, Blake Harmon, Bradley Walker, Claire "Cash Money" Price, CORO, David Bott, Deca, Desiree Godsell, Dicky Z, DJ Intel, DJ Rasta Root, Erin O'Donnell, Fahim Anwar, Greg Brunkalla, Isaac Ravishankara, James Pendergast, James Reitano, Jane McDormand, Jared Heck, Joe Fannon, Jorge Flores, Jorge "Northrock" Soto, Kavy Yesair, Konee Rok, KOOL AD, Lance Cantstopolis, Lucy and Ted Pease, Matt Sanphy, Mazadi Vision, Melissa Vargas, Mom and Dad, Michael Belcher, Mr. Complex, Northrock, Peggy McDormand, Pete Boyd, Raymond Long, Rew Kirst, Ryan Calavano, Rick Binelli, Robert Sims, Sang Yi, Sean Ferguson, Steven Fu, Taylor Swantek, Ted Pease, Tony Nicotera, Uncle Herm, Vinod Ponnusamy

Copy Editor: Melissa McDormand

FOR THE LOVE

For The Love: The Art of the Hip-Hop Video

Kevin McDormand

Pour L'Amour Books

www.pourlamourbooks.com

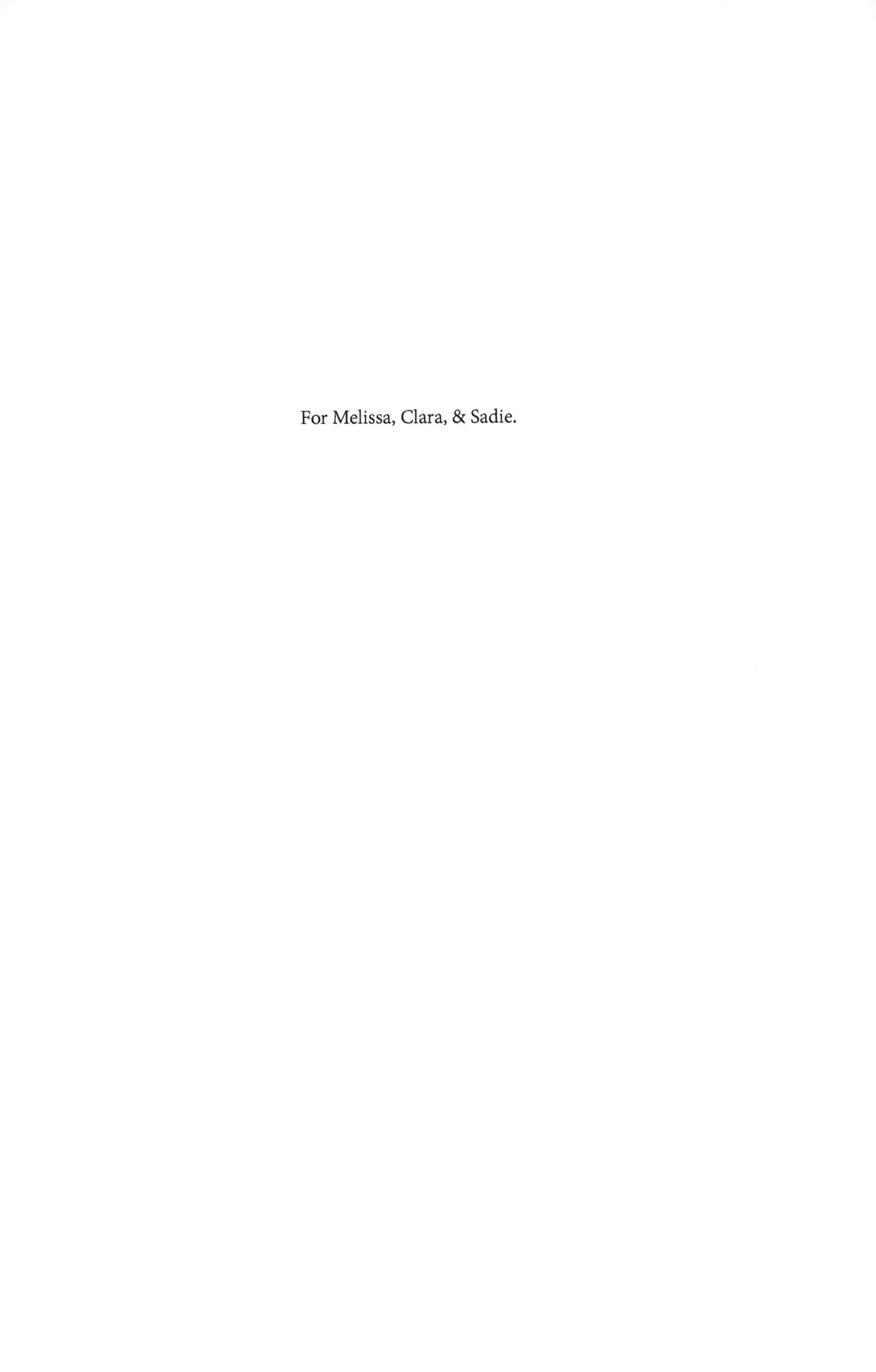

For Melissa, Clara, & Sadie.

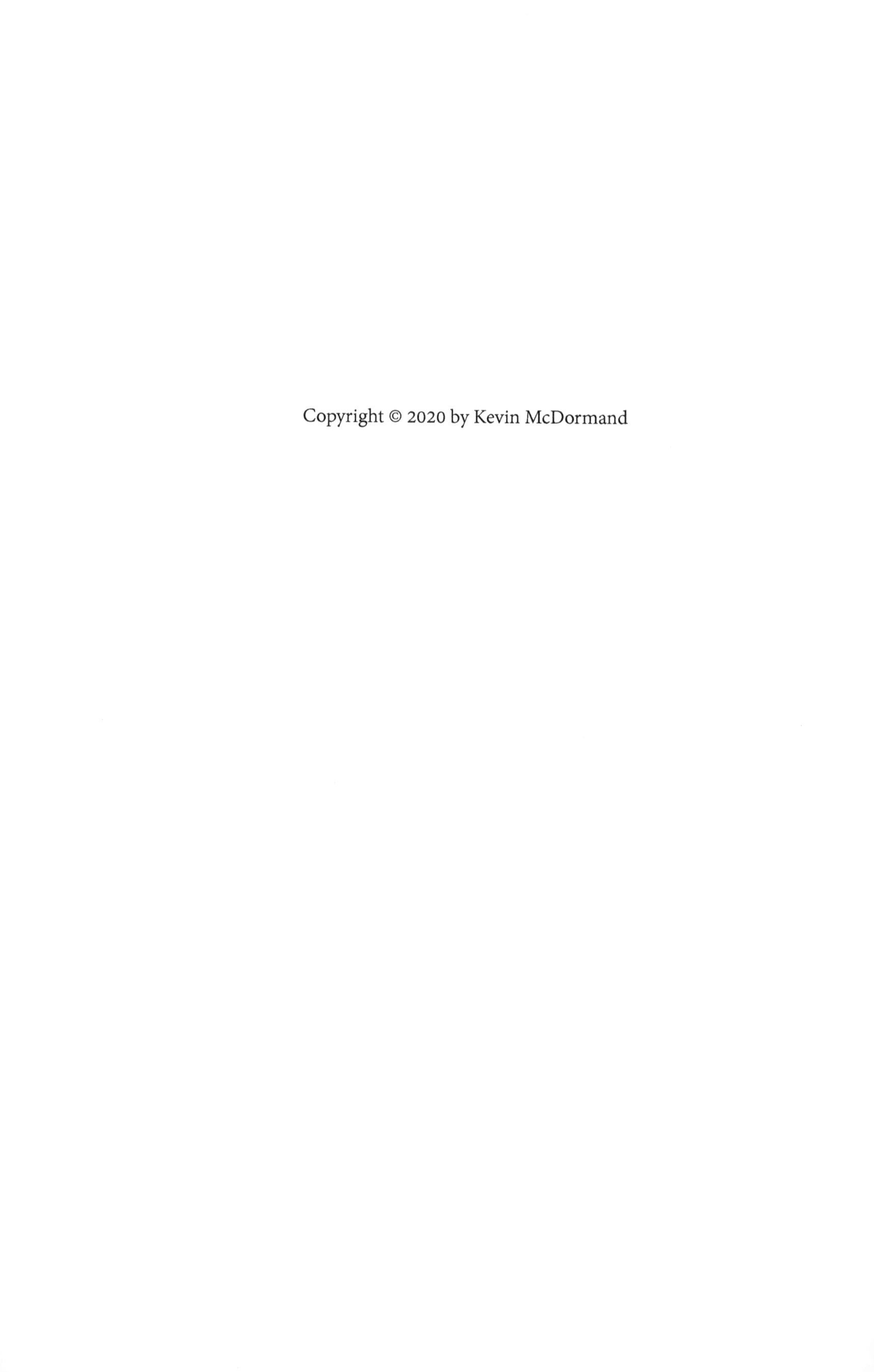

Author's note:

Each of these oral histories will be far more meaningful if you watch the video first. It may also be helpful to watch immediately after reading something that piques your interest. The beauty of our modern world is that each video is readily available on Youtube and can be accessed at any time.

CONTENTS

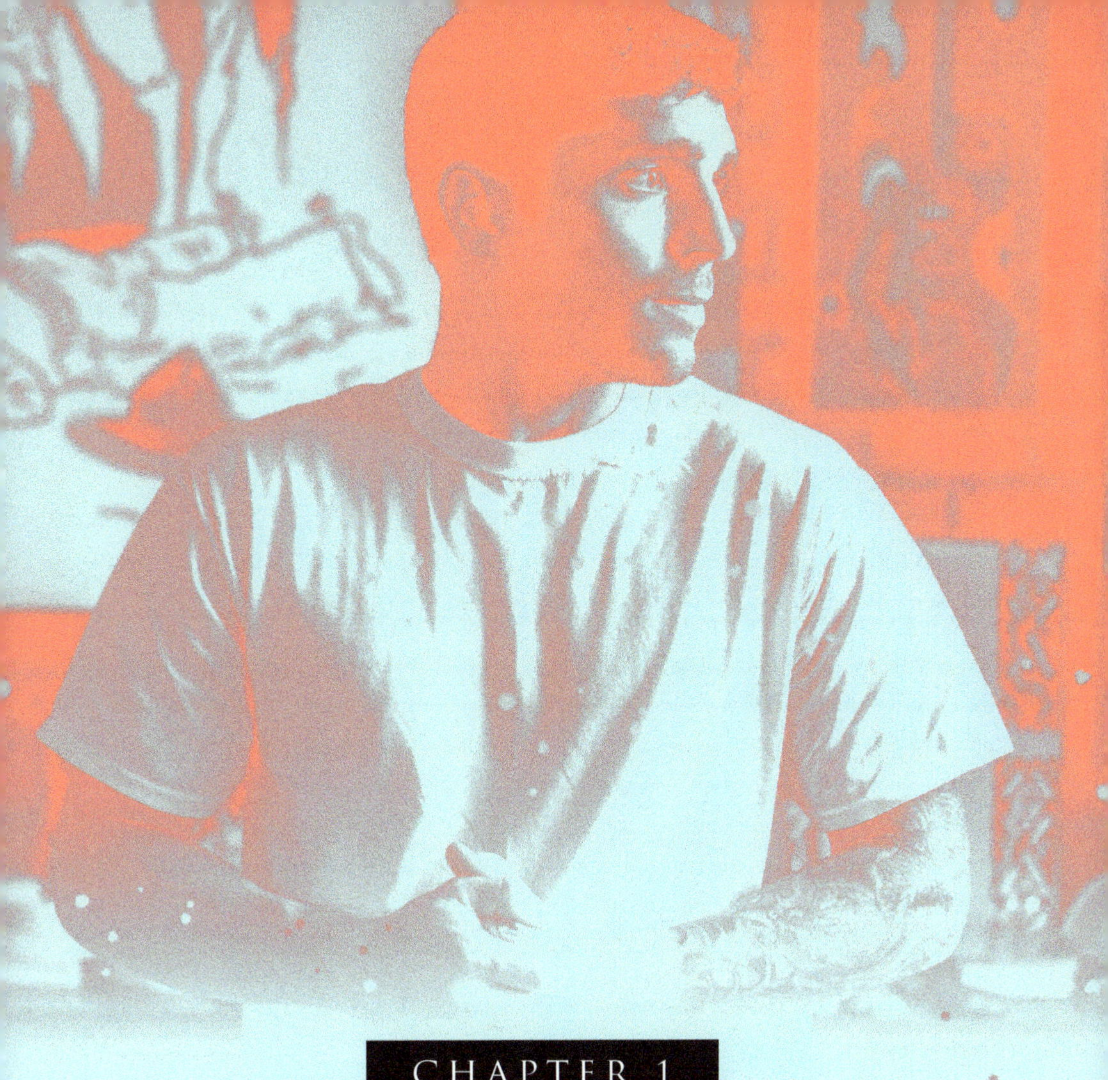

CHAPTER 1

DECA: WAITING

The following comes from an interview between Deca and me on November 15, 2017 about his video "Waiting, " in which Deca beautifully illustrates his impressive artistic versatility. Deca raps over a beat he produced. The beautiful video, featuring flower petals animated into living forms and geometric patterns, was animated and directed by Deca himself.

DECA, ARTIST/DIRECTOR:

It was kind of an interplay back and forth. I actually started the animation before the song. But then I did more of the animation once I had the song finished. It was a back and forth.

Even with writing and producing, I will do little bits back and forth and go between making the music and writing. So this was kind of a similar thing where I had a bouquet of old flowers that I gave my girlfriend and they were starting to wilt. One day, I started to pull the petals off, and messing around with animation. I had done little tests with animation but this was the first time that I actually tried a whole sequence. I did a sequence in twenty minutes building a mandala out of the petals. And that was the initial idea. Then, I animated a few of the sequences that I ended up using for the video. The song came after those first initial sequences. I saw that they fit well with the "Waiting" and then I started animating to the actual song.

Despite the experimental nature of "Waiting," Deca utilized most of what he shot.

DECA, ARTIST/DIRECTOR:

I'd say that 90% of what I made, I ended up using. I just did it on my phone actually. I got this cheap little stop motion app and did it all on the iPhone.

I think I did ten frames per second. And so however long the video is, I don't know, I am not good at math. (***Author's note: The video is 3:18, or 198 seconds. He shot roughly 1980 frames.)***

DECA, ARTIST/DIRECTOR:

Yeah, I did it over the course of two months I think. Maybe a little longer than that even. I would just decide, 'I'm going to animate tonight.' I would do it at night so I could control the light in my apartment. And then, I would just throw on music, animate for hours, and experiment. I would have loose ideas when I started animating of what I was gonna go for, but then a lot of times it would take a different direction as I was doing it. I'd say each segment was done in one night. So like the different parts that have a different look, whether it was black background or white background. I don't remember offhand how many there are, but maybe six or seven pieces. They were all done on different nights throughout the course of two or three months.

I actually haven't watched it in awhile but I know the part that starts at 0:42. That's probably my favorite animated sequence. I obviously chopped it up and used different parts but it was initially one sequence. I loved the morphing faces in this one.

BEST RAP VIDEOS THAT DO NOT FEATURE THE ARTIST (OR AN ANIMATED VERSION OF THEM)

Deca: Waiting (dir.: Deca)

Beastie Boys: Make Some Noise (dir.: Adam Yauch)

Gangrene: All Bad (dir.: Jason Goldwatch)

L'Orange f/ Blu: Alone (dir.: Ashton Blessing)

Makaveli: Hail Mary (dir.: Frank Sacramento)

Oddisee: Brea (dir.: Ryan Calavano)

The Brooklyn Doctors: The Couch Song (dir.: Mark Breese)

Watch The Throne: No Church In The Wild (dir.: Romain Gavras)

DECA, ARTIST/DIRECTOR:

The first animation test that I was telling you about, I did shortly after an ayahuasca ceremony. I think that experience definitely influenced the video. Part of my experience was very... something I don't want to go into too deeply, but it was an experience of the most beautiful, pure love. A vision of pure love and I saw this mandala with the softest pinks. Words can't even touch the experience. It was probably a week after. I was sitting at home and just for fun, started messing around with these flower petals. I made a shape with them and then thought, "Let me try to animate this." Petal by petal, trying to recreate something like what I saw in the Ayahuasca vision. So I was using all of these softer pink colors. What I made didn't actually end up in the video but that was kind of the start. The initial idea I think came from that experience. I'm a huge Bob Dylan fan. I listened to his whole catalogue from front to back probably twice while doing different segments. So listening to different music while I was animating definitely influenced what I was creating.

DECA, ARTIST/DIRECTOR:

There's a lot of old animation that I really like. I know that there's a million videos that I've seen that probably inspired me that I can't think of off the top right now. I love old Eastern European animation. Around the time I was doing this, and just in general, I'm inspired by a lot of that old animation. There's so much strange shit that came out in the 70's. There's this guy named Rein Raamat. His stuff is incredible. What is this other dude's name? Marcell Jankovics. You should check out a movie called Fehérlófia he directed. The most incredible animation and visionary stuff you've ever seen. These guys are just masters. The art I do, the art for the videos I collaborated with Steven [Mertens] on, and the Waiting video were definitely all inspired by watching a lot of old obscure animation.

COUSINS

DECA: SKYWARD

HOMEBOY SANDMAN: LIFE SUPPORT

MARCELL JANKOVICS: FEHÉRLÓFIA

Deca is incredibly versatile, a rapper, producer, and visual artist. Also a great word prefix, deca-, meaning ten. A decathlon has ten events, a decagon ten sides, and a decade ten years. Beware of words beginning with deca- that are derived from other prefixes, *decaf, decant, decay, decalcify, decapitate.* The number ten dominates our society. In sports, ten seconds is a knockout. There are ten bowling pins, and ten yards earns a first down. Most importantly, our society employs a base 10 system, where there are ten possible values for each place value. For example, you can have a 0, 1, 2, 3, 4, 5, 6, 7, 8, or 9 in each place value, (i.e. units, tens, hundreds, thousands, etc.) Each place value can be represented by 10 raised to some number.

10^0 = 1 (units place value)

10^1 = 10 (tens place value)

10^2 = 100 (hundreds place value)

10^3 = 1000 (thousands place value)

10^4 =10000 (ten-thousands place value)

And so on.

Rap music has greatly embraced the concept of The best songs for each value of x.

10^0: Ghostface Killah: One

10^1: Notorious B.I.G.: 10 Crack Commandments

10^2: The Game featuring Drake: 100

10^3: DJ Rude One featuring Shirt: 1K Dutches

10^4: Evidence: 10,000 Hours

10^5: Mac Miller: 100Grandkids (100grand kids = 100,000 kids)

10^6: Jay-Z: A Million and One Questions

10^7: Mack-10: Ten Million Ways

10^8: Birdman, Lil Wayne, Jeezy, Rick Ross: 100 Million

10^9: Rick Ross: Billionaire

10^{12}: Bun B featuring T-Pain: Trillionaire

10^0: Ghostface Killah:One: I have a theory called the Non-Crazy Argument Theory. It relies on the fact that many matters of taste are subjective. There is no right answer but some are altogether crazy. It is important that your subjective choice is above crazy. I developed this concept when discussing who was the best player in the NBA.[1] Some players were obviously not crazy- Giannis, Lebron, Steph, Harden, Durant. We had one name that we all decided was surprisingly not crazy. I threw out the name of Klay Thompson. While Klay is most likely not the best, we found his excellent defense and unselfish offensive role as evidence that you couldn't rule him out until seeing him in a lead scoring role. I went on this tangent to express the fact that "One" being the best song in rap is above crazy.

It's hard to pinpoint the apex of modern society but it may be contained within this song.

---

1 For timing purposes, roughly March of 2019.

Is it the beat, gifted by legendary Beatnut producer and sneaky-good rapper Juju? Is it the chorus: "Fifty cent sodas in the hood, they going crazy?" Is it the glorious ad libbed introduction, pieced together and culminating in "scream on it, Ghost?" All are candidates. One moment that is definitely not the apex is during the song's outro, when featured guest T.M.F. forgets how to talk shit. As the beat loops, ending each loop with a vocal "one," Ghost and guest cleverly riff, "We all connect as (One!)" Dope. "How many girls you got fucked? (One!)" Funny. "How many nuts you might bust? (One!)" Cool. "How many L's we smoke? (One!)" There the guest realizes he minimizes how much cool mairjuana smoking they do. "At a time!" Nice save, but that shit always cracks me up.

10^1: Notorious B.I.G.: 10 Crack Commandments: If I ever sell the movie rights to this book, I am paying DJ Premier a half million dollars to produce my album. DJ Premier is so dope that he almost made Fred Durst sound good.

10^2: The Game featuring Drake: 100: I've always been a bit neutral on Drake. I love some of his music but definitely less than the world does on average. But good lord is this song dope. Additionally, in spite of the fact that I suspect The Game and I would make the opposite decision in just about every life scenario, I have thoroughly enjoyed his catalog and feel he is criminally underappreciated. Additionally, my friends and I used to have a lot of fun freestyling while constantly mentioning iconic sneakers and rap personnel as an homage.

10^3: DJ Rude One featuring Shirt: 1K Dutches: In my younger days, Rude One and I rolled in the same circles. Now, he makes incredibly dope compilation albums. This is my favorite of his tracks. The best testament to Rude One's tastes is that his favorite baseball player is Eric Davis. Check his statline in 1987.[2]

10^4: Evidence: 10,000 Hours: Evidence, in the discussion for best emcee of the 10s, describes his growth in an homage to Gladwellian theory.

10^5: Mac Miller: 100Grandkids (100grand kids = 100,000 kids): No lie, I had never heard this song before searching for it while writing this. It's not bad at all though! Mac does well with numbers, as his "2009" is an all-timer.

10^6: Jay-Z: A Million and One Questions: Full disclosure: I went to boarding school. Why am I telling you this? I lived in a different room every year from 13 years old to 20 years old. If a song or album was dope enough, I can actually remember what room I was in when I rocked that song. Shout out to Evans Cottage, room 202, where I unapologetically played this song a million and one times.[3]

10^7: Mack-10: Ten Million Ways: Not only does this song feature a title connected to 10, but it is performed by Mack-10, member of legendary triumvirate Westside Connection. That has to mean something.

---

2 .297, 37HR, 50SB, 2nd in WAR.

3 In a weird twist, one of my best friends works at my alma mater and lives about 10 feet away from where my stereo was in November of 1997, when this dropped.

10^8: Birdman, Lil Wayne, Jeezy, Rick Ross: 100 Million: While most mistakenly think this song's title is money-related, it is actually a reference to how many dabs white kids have performed to it.

Also, let's put a little shine on producers Cool & Dre. "Boblo Boat," "From Adam," and "Hate It or Love It" are personal faves.

10^9: Rick Ross: Billionaire: He also made "Hood Billionaire" so you have to admire his consistency. Plus, it reveals that the exchange rate of regular to hood is 1 to 1 as a hood billionaire is a billionaire.

10^{12}: Bun B featuring T-Pain: Trillionaire: Did anyone think that T-Pain's music was going to age this well? I just read that T-Pain struggled with his Grammy nomination for "I'm on A Boat" as it rewarded a parody of his music over his actual music. I can't lie. I never considered that a parody. It was straight up hilarious but that can't minimize Pain's vocal skills. We all need to appreciate T-Pain.

Real question though. What white people are Bun B rolling with? "Go ask the whiteboys/ they say he's totally tubular." You sure they aren't ninja turtles in white people disguises?

DOPE SELF-DIRECTED VIDEOS

Beastie Boys: "Make Some Noise" & "So Whatchu Want" (Adam Yauch)

Deca: Waiting

Outkast: In Due Time (w/ Erykah Badu)

GZA: Shadowboxin'/4th Chamber

Jean Grae: Kill Screen

Brooklyn Doctors: The Couch Song (Mark Breese)

RZA: Tragedy

Gravediggaz: The Night the Earth Cried (RZA)

Tyler the Creator: Yonkers

CHAPTER 2

PHAROAHE MONCH: BROKEN AGAIN

AARONISNOTCOOL, WRITER & DIRECTOR, ON CONNECTING TO PHAROAHE MONCH:

I was at a media company called BKLYN 1834. It's been sort of put on pause. Currently, it's in restructuring. At the time, we were interested in being a content creator for artists that were up and coming. We wanted to make a splash with people and Pharoahe was a person who had seen a couple of our projects. And they were interested in working with us, so he came to our offices and played us three songs. "Broken Again" was the one I was taken most by. I was like "I want to make this one." He sent us these other ones that were going to be with Black Thought[4], but this was the one that emotionally got me going. I want to work on this one, so we started working on it.

AARONISNOTCOOL, WRITER & DIRECTOR, ON CREATING THE VIDEO'S TREATMENT:

I took a lot of inspiration from some of the words that he said in the song. I presented their team with a structure of how the story would go. The visual themes and the visual feeling of it. I got a response that was "I love it. Let's roll."

AARONISNOTCOOL, WRITER & DIRECTOR, ON A KEY REWRITE:

There's a lot of things that we wanted to do timewise that we didn't have time for. When I heard about smashing the glass, to me, it felt like the shot glass being put down and not necessarily glass smashing. That was the visual I wanted. You're smashing glasses. That's in you're taking a lot of shots, and in these moments, you begin to unravel. You are seduced by the addiction again.

"Broken Again" begins with a deliberate, slow moving shot beginning on a bathroom vanity and moving toward the protagonist's feet before cutting. The shot takes roughly 34 seconds, Cuaron-like in the music video world.

AARONISNOTCOOL, WRITER & DIRECTOR, ON THE STRIKING INITIAL SHOT:

That one was a deliberate shot where we wanted to introduce what you are about to see with the beginning of the song. So the drum comes in four times, and then the bass comes in. When the bass comes in, we begin to move. That was a very conscious thing that I wanted to do. Those four

4 Likely "Rapid Eye Movement," produced by Marco Polo.

things introduced production and titles. Then when we began moving, we introduced the scene that is meant to be confusing because you don't know why there's all this red tape on the floor, or why he's sitting down. And you can see his foot just tapping. That was also very important for us. We wanted it to feel like this isn't something…. we were very consciously playing the song for this moment. It was an intentional movement to introduce this song that way.

AARONISNOTCOOL, WRITER & DIRECTOR, ON THE VIDEO'S DISTINCT LIGHTING:

I was very inspired by the lighting of Fight Club. Jeff Cronenweth was the cinematographer there. He's done a lot of awesome work[5], and I was inspired by that kind of lighting where you just see little outlines of things. And that is very key to adding the surrealness when he's tripping or fiending. Those kinds of things were really important for me as I could show less and have room for things to be implied. I also felt that when things were a little bit lighter, I could have been less heavy-handed. But I did like certain moments. Especially in the bathroom and in the backdrop of the city where things sort of felt more free, and like there's an implication of things, but not necessarily being like "Oh, this is drug use."

AARONISNOTCOOL, WRITER & DIRECTOR, ON CHARACTER DEVELOPMENT:

A lot of people were praising Pharaohe for his talent and his ability to make a song that felt very real, and the work of us putting something together that wasn't such a blatant cautionary tale. But more something that feels like how a certain type of struggle might feel. We were very conscious about making Desiree[6], who plays the heroine, as attractive and relatable as possible. We wanted it to feel like this is someone you feel like you know. Who feels like she knows you. Why would you open your arms to her?

AARONISNOTCOOL, WRITER & DIRECTOR, ON CASTING AND DIRECTING DESIREE GODSELL:

She knew one of our producers. We were looking for somebody who had some dance experience because we wanted to have a sort of siren's dance. A couple of girls were brought forward. When we met Desiree, she was very talented and there was a warmness about her that really shined through once we started filming. I tried to explain to her what the dancer's going to be like. It wasn't until

5 Cronenweth was nominated for Academy Awards as Best Cinematographer for *The Social Network* and *The Girl with the Dragon Tattoo*. David Fincher also used Cronenweth on *Fight Club* and *Gone Girl*.

6 Desiree Godsell, professional choreographer to the likes of Santigold, also criss-crosses the world dancing salsa and bachata.

we put the music on and had her run through a couple of times to make sure you were on the same wave, on the same page, about how her dance would slowly begin to break down. And she would be more propped up by her bones. She was able to take that and run with it. She was brilliant.

THE VIDEOS OF NABIL ELDERKIN

During most interviews, I ask directors who inspires them or who they are a fan of. While that information helps me profile the director and their work, it also helps me to reexamine a director that I may have overlooked to some extent. When Aaron dropped the name Nabil Elderkin in our interview, it was familiar. I have always loved G.O.O.D. Music's "Mercy," directed by Elderkin. I watched Elderkin's catalogue and he's excellent. Some favorites:

G.O.O.D. Music, "Mercy:" Elderkin creates a nightmare parking garage street fight. Why is everyone wearing leather gloves? How many friends does this guy have lurking behind pillars? Did that guy just replicate? Why does that one guy have his own theme music? Jokes aside, Elderkin's "Mercy" takes the simple concept of disorientation and perfectly executes.

Bon Iver, "Holocene:" "Holocene" may be my favorite non-rap song ever. There, I said it. Holocene is a song about feeling small within the natural world. Elderkin could not have better executed that concept in his "Holocene" video. I don't even understand how this stunning, beautiful video is possible.

Alt-J, "Hunger of the Pine:" One of my favorite ten videos where the protagonist is struck by a barrage of arrows.

Just Blaze & Baauer f/ Jay-Z "Higher:" If you like the scene in Seinfeld when Kramer gets jumped by his karate classmates, this is the Elderkin for you.

The Foals "Late Night:" The cycle of life, darkly witnessed through the walls of the hotel the Foals perform in. Foals' guitarist Jimmy Smith later revealed that the man who hangs himself in the video nearly met his actual fate. "In the suicide scene the guy actually hung himself by mistake, which was pretty bonkers. We were watching it on the screens next door and it was really realistic, we thought he was doing an amazing job acting. Then he started clawing at the belt and went all limp. Nabil had his head in his hands and we all thought we had killed a Romanian dude."[7]

John Legend "P.D.A:" "P.D.A." perfectly illustrates the talent of Elderkin, as it is unlike his other videos, bright and a bit corny, but accomplishes everything it was designed to.

---

7 https://www.nme.com/news/music/foals-116-1262479

John Legend "Love Me Now": Elderkin's greatest strengths include highlighting groups and settings often overlooked by all of mainstream media while perfectly capturing the feel of the song. He touches upon all of his strengths here in this thoughtful piece.

Mike WiLL Made It f/ Kendrick Lamar, Rae Sremmurd, Gucci Mane "Perfect Pints:" My hunch is that Nabil lost the Famous Video Directors' Fantasy Football League, and the winner was allowed to pick 20 items that needed to be featured in his next video. By making them intentionally kitsch, Elderkin pulls off this wonder.

AARONISNOTCOOL, WRITER & DIRECTOR, ON THE INTIMATE SET:

There were a couple of more people there. Maybe two or three people to the side to assist, an AD and a producer were there. Other than that, we ran a really small group of people. There were never more than five people there on set. We knew what we wanted. We had a simple concept. It only took a couple of takes to get what we wanted from each thing. So once we had it, we just moved on.

AARONISNOTCOOL, WRITER & DIRECTOR, ON SCHEDULE:

It was two days of shooting. The first day was the dancing in the background of the city. The second day was the bathroom and the drinking scene. And then the scene where he's walking down the street.

AARONISNOTCOOL, WRITER & DIRECTOR, ON LOCATION:

We were working with this company who was trying to promote this top floor as a real estate thing. This was part of one of the things we were doing. They're in the "Special Thanks" credits. We had a month-long residency to do whatever we wanted there. One of the projects that we chose to do was to create a music video. It would be one of the spots in the video; an attractive spot.

AARONISNOTCOOL, WRITER & DIRECTOR, ON CREATING MEANING WITHIN THE VIDEO:

That's what we wanted to portray. The heroine that she is, in part, a savior but it's only a temporary thing. The savior is something that begins to eat away at him from the inside out. As soon as he begins to lose his strength and tries to keep her away, she then begins to embrace him. We wanted to make it clear that she was both initially a savior, but then it was something that could not be pushed away or shoved away. There's that scene where he's just trying to get her hands off of him. Then, we begin to see the darkness of the red tape be more present and more present. Then, the quiet moment of him looking down and his entire jacket is covered in red tape. We were going to use red paint, but it was going to be way too messy. It ended up working out well, because when we switched to red tape, we then wrote into the story that he would be able to remove it. We had shots of him removing it with nothing there. In the mirror, you could see that he was actually removing it in his mind. His mind's eye was showing him red tape, which was something heroin had left on him as he tried to remove himself from her.

When we were speaking about the heroine, I didn't equate it as the literal term for heroin as in the drug. I equated it as female hero. That's how I wanted to build her character. As his hero that sort of turns out to be a villain. From there, we started moving towards the "Broken Again" concept.

AARONISNOTCOOL, WRITER & DIRECTOR, ON WORKING WITH PHAROAHE MONCH:

This entire project was great. Everyone was really great to work with. Working with Pharoahe was a dream come true. I've been a fan of his for a long time. When he hit us up, I was like "we're obviously going to make a music video for him." It just depends which one. There was no way we weren't going to work with him. I was super excited about it. Once we started moving, once we started rolling, I felt like we connected really well. He brought a lot of energy that I didn't know we needed until we showed up and he brought it. Especially in the tape scenes because we needed him to be really vulnerable. That was day two of shooting. There were these things he was doing in the mirror that were distorting his face. I left a little bit in there as he's ripping away the tape. He was just making these faces, and I was like, "This is what it feels like. This is what he's bringing to the table of what it feels like to be strained and in pain." That was really special to see. He was a great guy to work with.

COUSINS:

PHAROAHE MONCH: BLACK HAND SIDE

DENTITIA AND SENE: RUNNIN.

SOFT GLAS: PERKS OF BEING A SUNFLOWER

229W43

The video bills the video's set as "229w43." I might be taking a leap but I believe this was filmed at 299 West 43rd Street, once known as The New York Times Building. Some facts that only I may find interesting:

4. Current tenants include Yahoo!, Snapchat, and Complex.

3. Jared Kushner owns the first 6 floors.

2. The building was purchased in 2004 for $175 million dollars and sold in 2007 for $525 million dollars. The math is too clean on that. The seller tripled his money in exactly 3 years.

1. The building also formerly housed Guy Fieri's Guy's American Kitchen and Bar, famously maligned in the New York Times by Pete Wells. A sampling:

"And when we hear the words Donkey Sauce, which part of the donkey are we supposed to think about?

Is the entire restaurant a very expensive piece of conceptual art? Is the shapeless, structureless baked alaska that droops and slumps and collapses while you eat it, or don't eat it, supposed to be a representation in sugar and eggs of the experience of going insane?"

In summary this building can be connected to the following media: Yahoo!, Snapchat, Complex, The Mueller Report, The New York Times, and most importantly *For The Love*.

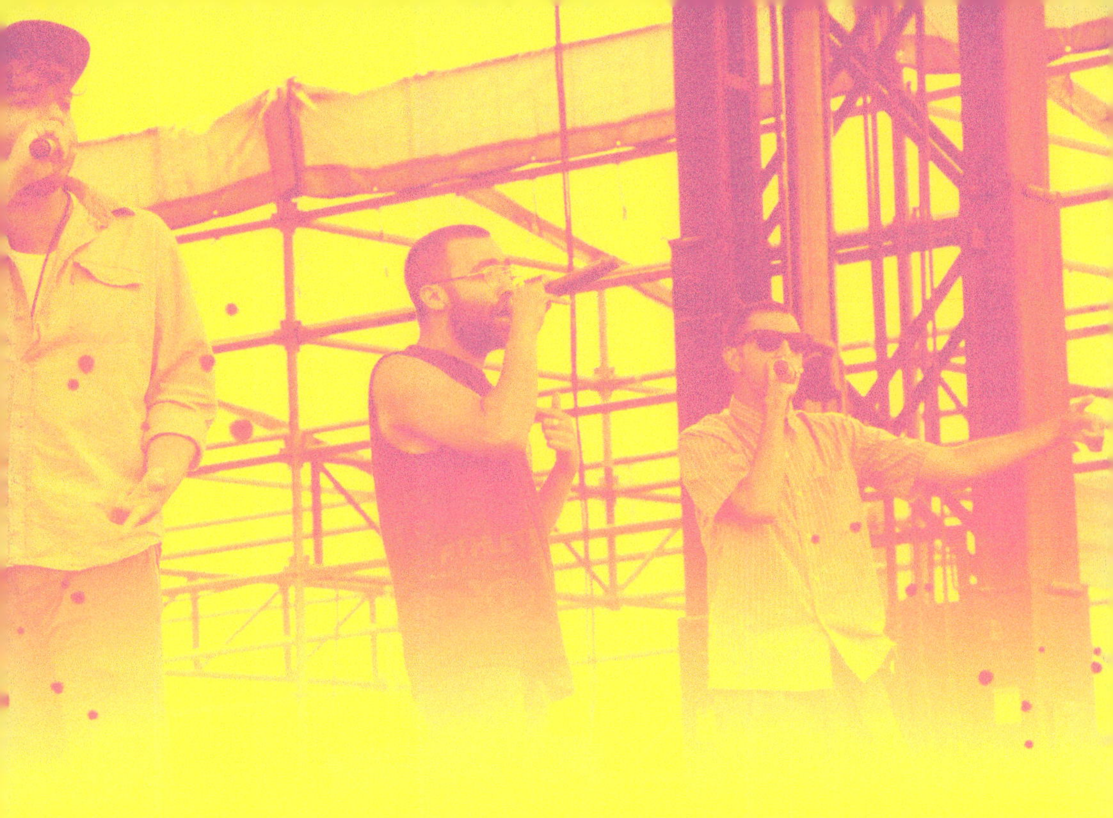

CHAPTER 3

DAS RACIST: GIRL

ARISTOTLE ATHIRAS, DIRECTOR:

Das Racist knew about our sketch group[8] by way of Hari Kondabolu[9], whose brother is in Das Racist[10]. Through Hari, they were aware of our group, and were fans, and we were talking to them for at least a year. Then, they did a concert in LA. I wasn't there but Fahim[11] and Hasan[12] went to go see them at the show. I can't remember how it came about, but they needed a video for "Girl," and somehow they landed on the idea that we would make it. We were going to try to put them in it, but it was a scheduling conflict as they were East Coast and we were West Coast. But they were like, "We trust you," and they got to see it before it came out. So if they didn't like it, it wouldn't see the light of day.

To this day I've only spoken to those guys. I've never met them. Hassan and Fahim had a tighter relationship with Heems, KOOL A.D., and Dapwell.

LANCE CANTSTOPOLIS, LEAD ACTOR:

Lance has always been a fan of Das Racist and hit Heems up on Twitter cuz wanted to dance in one of their videos. Even for split second. Always been dream of Lance to vibe and pelvic thrust in legit music video. Heems said, "Why don't you do whole video for "Girl?"" which of course much better situation as it now entirely Lance. Told Fahim and Aristotle and they thought would be good to fly under the Goatface banner and upload on our channel. All win for everyone. Lance get vehicle he always deserve, Das Racist get free music video, Goatface get to produce content that live on their channel and maybe siphon off some Das Racist fans.[13]

---

8 Goatface Comedy, consisting of Aristotle Athiras, Fahim Anwar, Hasan Minhaj, and Asif Ali. I recommend "Good Son," "The Truth," "Sanderson 720: Boston Manhunt" and "Spreadsheets," all available on Youtube.

9 Kondabolu justly murdered part of my childhood by creating *The Problem with Apu*, discussing the problematic nature of the *Simpsons* character.

10 Ashok Kondabolu, b/k/a Dapwell, is the most essential non-rapper/non-producer/non-DJ of all-time.

11 Fahim Anwar, who eerily resembles video star Lance Cantstopolis.

12 Hasan Minhaj, accomplished Goatface member, Daily Show senior correspondent, featured speaker at 2017 Correspondents' Dinner, Peabody Award Winner, host of Netflix's *Patriot Act*.

13 Lance's interview was conducted by email. All language and formatting is his own.

KOOL A.D., BEST RAPPER IN THE WORLD:

Hima[14] commissioned that one behind my back, I didn't know it was being made until it was done, I saw it and didn't really like it but let them drop it anyway.

ARISTOTLE ATHIRAS, DIRECTOR:

Before Goatface ever happened, me and Fahim were making sketches. We made this one sketch called 'Dirty Breakin.'[15] It's this trope of how dancing has a street vibe to it. I have a hard time articulating it, but we had this idea of this Van Damme type character trying to hit the dance world. We were hitting a lot of tropes with this video called 'Dirty Breakin.' If you watch it, it's the first time Lance (Cantstopolis) was ever on camera. I don't know if you've seen any of his other stuff, but he typically has an accent. But in this, he's just Fahim (Anwar.) He didn't really have an accent. We were brainstorming ideas for the *Girl* video. Fahim originally wanted to kind of do something that was a tribute to the Michael Jackson video or the videos where the guy is kind of trying to get at the girl.[16] The joke is that in real life, it's a creepy thing. This person following you wherever you go. Could we use the Lance character and insert him as a plug and play thing? He didn't even have a name at the time.

LANCE CANTSTOPOLIS, LEAD ACTOR:

He good director. He have good eye and know what he want. Sometimes he use too much fog on set, but it look good in the edit so cannot complain.

ARISTOTLE ATHIRAS, DIRECTOR:

Fahim has a friend. They both came up with the name Lance when he started doing this character on stage. Before that, he was just "Dirty Breakin" van Damme. We just inserted him into the idea we had for the Girl video. It's kind of this joke about this guy who's obsessed with this girl. If you take the tropes you see in all of these music videos and you apply them to real life situations, how it really plays out. That's what we were making fun of.

---

14 Himanshu Suri aka Heems. Das Racist emcee. Heems now releases solo efforts and tracks as a member of Swet Shop Boys with Riz MC and producer Redinho.

15 Check for SNL's Melissa Villaseñor.

16 Young bloods, please watch Michael Jackson's "The Way You Make Me Feel."

THE ODD DRAW OF SINGER KOOL A.D.

There was KOOL A.D. before Das Racist. At one time, he played synth and wrote lyrics for Boy Crisis, who he described as "Brian Emo and Timbaland's love child."[17] Popular enough to be featured in the New York Times[18], they were not universally lauded. A Pitchfork writer called them "the absolute worst band in the world right now. Seriously. Think of every awful cliché about Williamsburg hipster douchebags, then multiply them by 100. Then take those clichés and have them play ironic 'smoove' white boy electro r&b."[19] While their anticipated album was never released, KOOL A.D. brought some pop vocal sensibility to the world of hip-hop.

On "Girl," Kool A.D. is a passably good pop vocalist who knows how little he needs to do to bolster the incredibly catchy BloodPop production. A.D. and Francis Starlite[20] duet on "It's Alrite 2 Cry." While AD does not seem as comfortable on it as he does on "Girl," the song is a resounding success.

No discussion of KOOL A.D. vocals is complete without a discussion of the uniquely voyeuristic and eventually problematic "Prove It." Once upon a time, "Prove It" was complicated- but in a good way. While not the first love song from the perspective of an imperfect partner, "Prove It" never felt like it was a story. It felt like a view into the artist's newly hopeful soul in opposition to his usually subversive, personally-private, and at times, silly material. Finally, the song culminates in KOOL A.D.'s most sincere and effective singing, "I will be good to you baby. I can do it. I can do it. And you looked me in the eye and said 'Prove it. Prove it.'"

"Prove It" took on a different feel in 2018. Four women, including KOOL A.D.'s estranged wife Saba Moeel, accused the musician of sexual assault. Is the love interest in "Prove It" Moeel? If she is fictional, some part of the character must be based on her. "Prove It," which once felt like an imperfect partner describing the call that forced him to be a better man, now feels like a man romantically waxing on his partner hoping to be treated better while you already know the eventual outcome.

I struggle now with my relation to A.D.'s music. In all honesty, I have not been able to totally withdraw as I did with R. Kelly.[21] At the moment I was alerted to the news of the accusations against A.D., I was talking about Das Racist and its members among friends as much as any other artists. Often, I find myself sneaking a listen to "Leverage" or "Pass the Milk" and feeling weird about it. And then there's "Prove It." In spite of the history and maybe because

---

17 www.theguardian.com/music/2008/nov/21/boy-crisis

18 www.nytimes.com/2009/09/06/arts/music/06play.html

19 www.pitchfork.com/features/article/7542-iceland-airwaves-festival/

20 Of Francis and the Lights

21 Yes, even "Ignition (Remix)"

of the history, I find myself compelled to listen. Why do we watch videos of fistfights and flock to podcasts about serial killers? How will we rationalize our relationships with the art of people who have faced troubling accusations- Bill Cosby, Robert Kelly, Mike Tyson, Tim Allen, Mel Gibson, Phil Spector, Kobe Bryant?

LANCE CANSTOPOLIS, LEAD ACTOR:

Song grew on Lance.[22] Kind of fucking weird song at first cuz so unconventional but it get doper and doper and you understanding the layers. Yeah, danced to song for quite a while filming cuz multiple takes and stuff but never got tired of it and still was fresh enough to squeeze dope moves out of.

In spite of the intended creepiness of Girl, a moment borders on tenderness.

ARISTOTLE ATHIRAS, DIRECTOR:

Are you talking about the MySpace add? The facebook add? (laughing at self) MySpace add? It was my apartment I just moved into. Actually, I hadn't moved in yet. I just had my keys to it. It was all empty and we had this open space. I honestly can't recall how we landed on the idea of adding her on Facebook.

ARISTOTLE ATHIRAS, DIRECTOR:

Goatface is such a collaborative thing with all of us throwing ingredients in the mix. Sometimes you can't recall how. With Lance, if you watch "Dity Breakin," Fahim actually had those extensions sewn into his hair. Those were permanent for a few months.

ARISTOTLE ATHIRAS, DIRECTOR:

Later on, when we started doing more stuff with the character, we got a clip-on that he could clip in. Originally, it was sewn into his hair.

---

22 The secret to unearthing great hip-hop is to check for the producer. In most cases, their importance outweighs that of the emcee. For that reason, I obsessively check who produces every rap song I enjoy. While writing this article and watching the video for the ten-millionth time, I realized that I had no idea who produced it. A quick trip to Genius told me that it was BloodPop, who I had never heard of. His top produced songs at time of writing included Justin Bieber's "Sorry," Hailee Stainfeld's "Capital Letters," and Lady Gaga's "Million Reasons."

ARISTOTLE ATHIRAS, DIRECTOR:

For me as a director, I'm really into preparation. Knowing what we're going to shoot. Getting a solid idea and then improvising beyond that. Fahim for the most part, when it comes to dancing, does not like choreographing it beforehand. Dance specifically, I personally like to be prepared. He puts me in this corner. The scene in the dance studio that we cut back and forth with, I kept him going over and over again until I felt like I had what I needed. We're shooting a lot of this dirty so... he did a lot of dancing, if that's what you're asking. There were some times with some heavy breathing.

ARISTOTLE ATHIRAS, DIRECTOR:

Fahim? He is pretty athletic. He has natural born athleticism. He's really good at basketball. He has a natural ability to dance too which is some shit that I don't have. I can dance if I practice, but I can't fuckin improvise a dance like he can. He just goes all out.

LANCE CANTSTOPOLIS, LEAD ACTOR:

Yeah, crazy huh? Pretty accomplished even though not having any awards. Not sure dude. Lance hear music and just go. There no school I go to or lessons I take. It all feeling from bones when tunes get into ear and brain. Lance a passenger to the groove. Like in the back of an Uber and dancing like driver named Armin who ask if you need cell phone charger.

Every great love interest music video needs both the pursuer and the pursued. While Lance excelled in the former role, things fell into place when the video landed Hayley Marie Norman for the latter. Hayley, an accomplished actress, is best known to me as the woman who makes it with Will Smith in Hancock.

ARISTOTLE ATHIRAS, DIRECTOR:

She was a friend of... or she was in... I can't remember who knew her? If it was Fahim or Asif... It wasn't me. I didn't know Hayley. The first time I met her was that day. I think Hasan may have met her on a show. We kind of asked if she would do it. Don't tell Hayley that we had potential backups if she wasn't interested in doing it. But luckily she was. She was perfect for it.

LANCE CANTSTOPOLIS, LEAD ACTOR:

Not like we kicking it all the time and shit. She cool but very much live and die that day shooting "Girl." She busy actress doing ton of stuff. Our path cross in space time but never since. She cool tho.

ARISTOTLE ATHIRAS, DIRECTOR:

In LA, it frequently boils down to if you have friends that in the business, you can kind of ask. Even if they have agents, you can reach out to them about being in your thing, and sometimes they will, sometimes they won't.

Like all good music videos, "Girl" was filmed guerilla-style. No permits, no permission.

ARISTOTLE ATHIRAS, DIRECTOR:

It was all filmed in LA. The first shot was in Koreatown where Fahim and I used to live. The fountain was shot at the apartment building that Hasan lived in. The library shots were in the UCLA library. Moments after we got the shot, we got kicked out. We rented the dance studio out. Same dance studio we rented for "Dirty Breakin." We rented it out again. It's off of Highland in Santa Monica.[23]

LANCE CANTSTOPOLIS, LEAD ACTOR:

The fountain Lance come out of was in Hasan Minhaj's apartment complex in LA. He in Goatface so helped out with shoot. Library scene was at UCLA library. Last shot was in Aristotle's apartment.

"Girl" is almost entirely dedicated to Lance's pursuit of Hailey. The pursuit takes a short break as Lance ends a mysterious scuffle with an acrobatic roundhouse kick.

ARISTOTLE ATHIRAS, DIRECTOR:

A lot of those actors are comics and comedians who are friends of ours. I've been wanting to shoot a fight scene like that for a long time. I remember having our meetings and saying "How do we get this fight scene I've been wanting to shoot for a while?" So, that's how that happened. That was in the parking lot of the apartment building we used to live in. In this little tucked away corner. I just smoked the whole place and then starting lighting it.

23 I'm about 90% sure this was filmed at the Hollywood Dance Center.

LANCE CANTSTOPOLIS, LEAD ACTOR:

Only protection in place was TRUST. Lance assure actors would not kick in face. Proud to say good to my word. No faces were harmed in shooting.

While filming "Girl," Athiras discovered a perk of shooting a music video instead of his typical day shooting sketch comedy.

ARISTOTLE ATHIRAS, DIRECTOR:

That did happen quite a bit, but since this is a music video, you can't fuck up a shot by laughing really loud because you're not getting audio. That has happened in the past. There were times where I was shooting *The Truth* with Hasan Minhaj. There is a reason a lot of those are jump cuts. I shot them all. Except for one of them. The reason why there are so many jump cuts is because I would lose my composure and laugh at something he said.

In spite of the success of "Girl," Athiras hasn't attempted to replicate his success with another foray in the music video world.

ARISTOTLE ATHIRAS, DIRECTOR:

I have worked on other music videos but they weren't mine. I kind of consulted on them. Two others. They were these starter artists. They don't have a career yet. This is the only one that got air time. And I'm proud of it. It was a really fun experience. A lot of times when I would shoot a sketch, I had to wear so many hats. I'm trying to make sure people shut the fuck up and do what they're supposed to be doing, so they don't fuck up my audio so I get the shot I need. I storyboard everything, so I need this shot, this shot, this shot. Balancing so many spoons on my nose, but with the music video so much of it was already taken care of. Your score and your audio is all done. I don't have to do shit except shoot. That's fun. That's also what makes music videos so easy is that you don't have to have continuity. You can shoot some cool shit and see how it lays with the music.

COUSINS

DAS RACIST: MICHAEL JACKSON

GOATFACE: DIRTY BREAKIN'

SWET SHOP BOYS: AAJA

GREAT MOMENTS IN SUBVERSIVE HIP-HOP: THE DAS RACIST "SELECTOR" FREESTYLE

Das Racist consisted of emcees KOOL A.D. and Heems along with non-emcee Dapwell. The two rappers are generally considered to be of the highest caliber; funny, well-read, super intelligent, unique. Dapwell was sort of the same, but he didn't rap. He served as a hype man, dancer, and muse.

All three members sought to subvert the ideals of hip-hop. When the typical indie rap act books *Conan,* they perform their hit as true to the original, as polished as possible, in their finest clothes in front of bright lights. When DR books Conan, they play an experimental version, programmed live, in what they were wearing in the dark.[24]

Still, as a fan of all things subversive, I prefer their *Selector* appearance to this performance.

The world of hip-hop has long romanticized the freestyle as a sort of dual threat marketing ploy/demonstration of requisite skills. On radio shows, mixtapes, and videos, rappers kick a freestyle that ranges from 0 to 100 percent pre-written. Typically, they do what they need to pass the test. The most gifted freestylers can be more instinctive, while the rest blur some edges to make their memorized line seem spontaneous.

Regardless, these freestyles often have high stakes, and emcees work hard to make an impression.

Das Racist, when still emerging, landed a feature with prestigious Pitchfork for their "Selector" freestyle series. As you can imagine, the typically cheeky trio took it seriously and showed their incredible lyrical chops.

---

24 I highly recommend watching this.

Actually, they were incredibly creative but only in their subversion, but not their lyrics as much.

See, Pitchfork was surely hoping to get a couple of minutes of freestyle from super-clever emcees KOOL A.D. and Heems, flanked by Dap's legendary energy. Instead, they got:

40 seconds of Heems freestyling as his bandmates cackle and giggle.

KOOL A.D. mustering the following four lines:

"Michael Jackson, a million dollars, feel me? Holla!

Michael Jackson, a million dollars, feel me? Holla!

Michael Jackson, a million dollars, feel me? Holla!

Michael Jackson, a million dollars, feel me? Holla!"[25]

Dap, the non-rapper, rapping for 40 seconds. This includes the punchline "Take your dad to work day is what this is."

Das Racist's critically acclaimed rappers: 40 seconds of freestyle.

Das Racist's non-rapping comedian: 40 seconds of freestyle.

Arguably, this feature could have helped to make or break the emerging trio. In thinking like the most incredibly subversive entity in rap history[26], DR did what everyone wanted, by doing what no one wanted.

---

25 This line became the chorus of their amazing track *Michael Jackson*. I will discuss this video in a future volume!

26 Apologies to Kool Keith and Prince Paul.

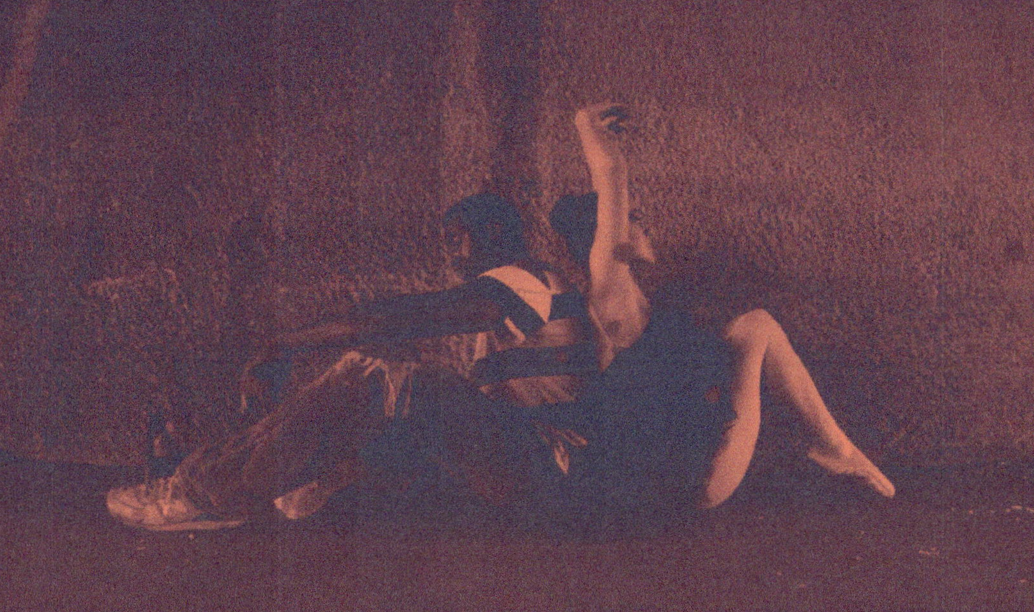

CHAPTER 4

ODDISEE: BREA

RYAN CALAVANO, DIRECTOR:

I've done videos with Open Mike Eagle[27] for a while. Oddisee's on Mello Music[28], plus he's one of my favorite artists so I hit up Mike Mello, owner of Mello Music group, and was like "Yo! Is Oddisee doing anything?

Oddisee[29] is always doing something. At that time, he was set to release his 12-track "Odd Tape," a collection of instrumental music.

RYAN CALAVANO, DIRECTOR:

I got the beat tape[30] that Oddisee was putting out before it came out and it was basically like "Hey, pick a track and if anything comes to you, any creative thoughts going on, let me know." I heard *Brea* and it was like an instant vibe, like slow moving black and white. I'm a beat guy. I used to make beats and I always wanted to be a producer. I'm just a fan of producers and that beat was so filthy. I kind of had that initial thought of doing that juxtaposition between a homeless person and a ballerina in the streets. That was my initial thought. I talked to Mike from Mello Music[31] and Oddisee[32]. Once I got Oddisee on the phone, it was dope like, "I can't believe I'm talking to Oddisee!" I said, "This was my concept, What do you think?" He was like, "Yo, go ahead!"

Unlike most rap videos, Ryan's vision of "Brea" was not following Oddisee around with a camera. His vision was a narrative, and he needed to cast two dancers in starring roles.

---

27 Calavano's video for Open Mike Eagle's *Celebrity Reduction Prayer* is a must-watch.

28 If Mello puts it out, it's dope. My Spotify playlist is chock full of their artists, namely Oddisee, Apollo Brown, Open Mike Eagle, L'Orange, Denmark Vesey, and Gensu Dean.

29 Oddisee might be the most impressive artist that is not known to all music fans. As I write this, I fear that I may have to edit every sentence that I write, as he should have reached common consciousness already and could at any moment. Please listen to these songs immediately: Camera, That's Love, Own Appeal, Miami, Belong To The World, When I Stopped Looking.

30 The Odd Tape

31 I listen to so much Mello Music on Spotify that they might actually make meaningful money from my streaming.

32 Like, I probably bought Oddisee somewhere between a Chipotle meal (with Chips and Guacamole) and a nice hoodie last year.

RYAN CALAVANO, DIRECTOR:

I met Taylor at a photoshoot. I was doing behind the scenes for this yoga pants company. She has an amazing look and she was in ballerina stuff at that shoot. I was like "I got this concept." Because I had the concept and was looking for people, asking friends. My go-to dancer wasn't available, so let's see what's up with Taylor. She was down. She's like the coolest chick ever. Was down for whatever.

TAYLOR SWANTEK[33], DANCER:

Ryan was filming behind the scenes at a photoshoot for an athletic wear brand. That's where we met. We got to talking and he said, 'I have a shoot coming up, what styles of dance do you do?" He mentioned that it was for a music video that he was going to be directing and asked if I would be interested. I sent him some of my work and we got to emailing from there. I fell in love with the song and I loved his concept for the video. Ryan is insanely talented and so fun to work with, we've stayed in touch and I've been fortunate enough to work with him again since Brea. His enthusiasm on set is infectious.

RYAN CALAVANO, DIRECTOR:

I met Jason[34] because I work for Aloe Blacc[35] every once in a while. I met him in the studio because they are old school friends. We were just talking about dancing and whatnot. I just had this concept in the back of my head. "Yo, send me a video or something that you got!" He's super old school, kind of 90s hip-hop dance. He runs a little studio[36] where people come and just do freestyle dancing and whatnot. I was just like, "This is perfect." The two together would be amazing. We just

---

33 Taylor is not some amatuer dancer that Ryan tracked down at a photo-shoot. She is incredibly accomplished. You can catch her at Taylor Swift's right shoulder at the end of the "Shake It Off" video.

34 The lead male role was filled by Jason Ulysses, a freestyle and hip-hop dancer, dance instructor, radio host and documentarian. You can find two of his films, "Freestyle: The Beginning of the End" and " Show and Prove: A Freestyledance Experience" on Youtube.

35 I used to work for a small record label. We had some business dealings with another small label. They signed a duo called Emanon. The two members were amazingly dope producer Exile (Blu, Fashawn, much more) and Aloe Blacc (I played Green Lights at my wedding.) If I remember correctly, their 2002 EP with that label sold a few thousand copies. The music industry has this weird world where if you discover an artist too early, it gets you nowhere. It's counterintuitive.

36 Rosemen Visual Dance, 2920½ West Florence Ave, Los Angeles, CA.

did one day of rehearsal, the day before the shoot. There's no choreography or anything. I was just like, "I'm gonna let you guys work."

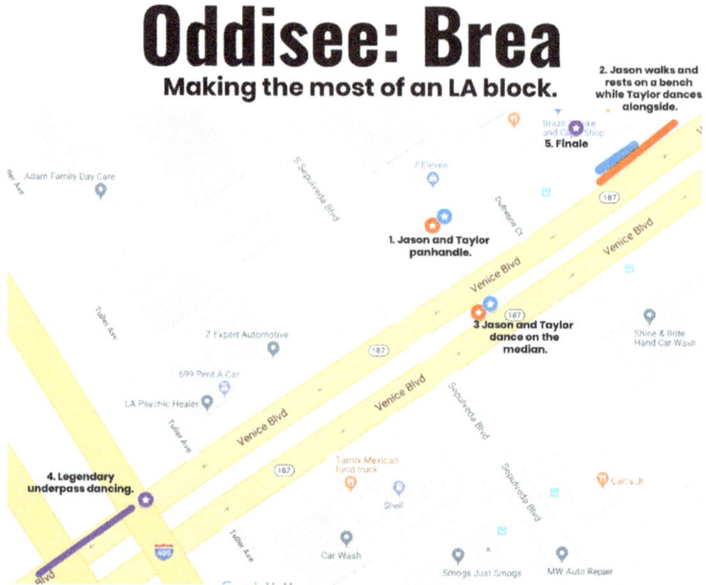

TAYLOR SWANTEK, DANCER:

Ryan, Jason, and I met one time before we filmed to rehearse, but it was pretty loose. Nothing was set. That was one of the things going into it that was interesting because it was very much about the locations we were in. We were following the music all the way through this narrative that Ryan had created that was so beautiful and so interesting. The narrative fit the song perfectly but the scenes still left a lot of room for us to get creative with our interpretation of our characters. We had all met up at Jason's studio to get to talk in person and feel each other's energy; to talk about the ideas behind the story, the layers in the song, different points in the music that we wanted to highlight, where we were going to shoot it, and the timeline of the shots for the shoot day.

RYAN CALAVANO, DIRECTOR:

During the shoot, it was like, "Here's the scenario. You guys just interact in this way at this point." That's how it all came together. I got so lucky with those two because basically I was like "Yo, do your thing and we'll shoot it and see what's going on." It was amazing.

TAYLOR SWANTEK, DANCER:

It was a small crew. We all met up, got our wardrobe set, and the four of us started walking around the streets of Venice[37] to review the locations that Ryan had scouted. We just started filming and going from there. Ryan was directing us throughout, but he really let Jason and I run with it. It was so cool to have that kind of freedom. I think Jason and I got into a really great flow with each other, playing off each other in different ways with me trying to absorb and mirror his emotional ups and downs. In a way, I felt like at times I was trying to be his cheerleader, his spirit, and keep him in a good place. At other times, I was watching over him, seeing what he felt and experienced on his journey and absorbing those emotions when he felt down and frustrated.

RYAN CALAVANO, DIRECTOR:

Brea's pretty much just the name of the song and it just so happens I'm about 5 blocks away from La Brea. A lot of people are like, "Where'd you shoot this?" I live in West LA and all these locations are within 2 miles of my house. My friends make fun of me because I shoot near my house because it's easy and it's less money and travel. What happened was, I was riding my bike to work and I would ride a trail all the way on that little river, the mini LA River in Culver City. I would ride by those palm trees and the Culver City River with the concrete every day. I'm like, "I got to shoot there for sure." Then, the night part with all the lights in the convenience store, that's right by my house. I walked by at night. There's all these locations. "I'm going to shoot there. There's going to be some point where I'm going to shoot at these locations," and it all kind of worked out. We shot it all in one day, 2 hours here, 2 hours there. Got it all done in 6 or 7 hours.

TAYLOR SWANTEK, DANCER:

I feel like that's the one thing about being in LA. Dancing on the sidewalk in a tutu is not the most unusual thing. Most people have seen that type of thing here because there are always people running around filming. We definitely had some people coming up and trying to see what was going, but there really weren't that many people around, so it wasn't that much of an issue. In the shot where we were in front of the laundromat, there were a few people inside cleaning up before they closed for the night. Watching the video back again this morning, I noticed you can actually see two of them watching us from inside. For the most part, people were really respectful with what was going on. They were intrigued, but would walk by us and just watch a little bit and walk away.

---

37 California, not Italy. Venice, Italy doesn't have streets.

RYAN CALAVANO, DIRECTOR:

It's so important because our budgets are crazy. We literally had six hundred bucks to do this whole thing. Maybe it was $1,000 and I spent it all on talent. It's about finding those locations that you won't get kicked out of immediately and are amazing.

TAYLOR SWANTEK, DANCER:

It was a fusion of styles. There are balletic elements but we were definitely breaking that form. I had a lot more fluidity and looseness with my upper body than typical if I was just doing classical ballet, and I completely let go of my technique in some moments. Seeing Jason's whole vibe and his moves, I tried to incorporate some of that style as well. If I was describing it to another dancer, I don't know that I have an exact term. I would mostly describe it as ballet fusion.

RYAN CALAVANO, DIRECTOR:

We implemented some real live 8 millimeter lenses for that shot under the bridge. The way that'd set up there's a lot of depth lines and perspective. Also, we had that on a Ronin[38] with a Steadicam. We could kind of move and they do a lot of swooping motions. There's a lot of run and gun stuff so we were just switching lenses, getting a shot, switching lenses, getting shots, and seeing what's good. I had kind of a basic idea of what I wanted to get at that point. It made sense for me to go a little wider to give it a more interesting look.

TAYLOR SWANTEK, DANCER:

When we were shooting the part under the freeway overpass, a fire truck came through the tunnel and honked the horn. We were so immersed in our dancing at that moment that we were pretty startled as the horn echoed through the tunnel.

If you casually watch "Brea," you may miss the one to two second art pieces spliced throughout the video.[39] *I could describe them as a moving triple exposure but I strongly prefer the words of Ryan and Taylor.*

---

38 The DJI Ronin is a camera platform that uses motors to stabilize video, even when shot in a less than steady manner.

39 1:28, 2:02, 2:38, 3:34, 5:15, credits.

RAP VIDEO'S BEST DANCING (IN NO PARTICULAR ORDER)

- Swantzek & Ulysses in Brea.
- RA the Rugged Man, Lessons (2:17)
- MC Hammer, U Can't Touch This
- Gittin' Funky by Kid N' Play
- Let's Get it by G. Dep
- Salt & Pep in Push It
- The one dance move in So Fresh, So Clean
- The Way You Move
- Gossip Folks
- Never Catch Me by Flying Lotus
- Girl by Das Racist
- Sunday Candy by the Social Experiment
- Hip Hop Hooray
- Benz or Beamer
- Put Your Hands Where My Eyes Can See
- Hip-Hop by dead prez
- Bring the Pain
- Swervin by Fat Tony
- Aaja by Swet Shop Boys

RYAN CALAVANO, DIRECTOR:

The green screen with the multiple? I've been doing stuff like that for years now, because basically the cheapest way to shoot stuff is on green screen. Then, you do whatever you want with it. First and foremost, I knew I wanted to implement some sort of element like that, so we shot Taylor dancing on the screen. We shot Jason on the green screen, too, but we didn't end up using it. Her movement is unbelievable. Putting her on top of two or three other images of herself. I knew what it could look like because I had that in the chamber. I had done some other stuff with ballerinas in green screen and I was like "that's going to go in it somehow."

TAYLOR SWANTEK, DANCER:

The video was primarily the four of us walking around shooting on the spot and it turned out so beautifully. The scenes where it's a black background, Ryan did incredible visual effects. Alternating the speed, ramping up and down, overlapping with different movements that he spliced into a couple places... That was shot in his garage studio at the end of the day. We did this all in one day. After sunset, we finished getting all of our exterior shots, and he was like, "Let's do some other stuff to mix in." That was a really fun part, when we were just in there with the green screen, cheering each other on like, "Okay, go for it! Freestyle this. Think about it like that." Ryan was calling cues out to us, "So imagine you're really sad. How are you going to show that with your upper body? Now you're elated." He would play the track, and we would just groove and experiment. Jason and I had heard it a thousand times by then. With a song like Brea, you don't get tired of listening to it. It's such a rich musical tapestry and resonates with you so deeply. It's just such a vibe. I still love that song and now hearing it always takes me back to those moments. We had a great time shooting together and having this improvised jam session to end the day was amazing. Jason had some epic moves, but I think Ryan chose to just use the shots of me because my character was kind of the ethereal spirit.

Ryan's vision included a poignant final scene that, in practice, was bolstered by the incredibly soulful acting of Ulysses and Swantek. The final product was the rare piece of art that turns out better than the artists anticipate.

RYAN CALAVANO, DIRECTOR:

Initially, I went back and forth on whether to make that black and white. The idea behind the relationship between Jason and Taylor blossoms and changes. It turns from gloomy to beautiful by the end of it. They're almost comfortable with each other at the end. It becomes more real, not like Taylor is a spectre or a soul. A lot of people sort of think she represents his soul, which is sort of correct. It's more like a two dimensions sort of thing. She represents his soul on a couple levels. With color, it looked amazing. That's part of it. I'm kind of a practical director too. Sometimes, you make plans and you break them because some shit looks better than what you actually planned. I also like taking the way things are done and if I have a way to change it or do something different, I like to think of that. Even if it's considered wrong or inconsistent. That's just another way to make it more dynamic.

TAYLOR SWANTEK, DANCER:

The laundromat scene is one of my favorites. I know Ryan was really excited about that. He had driven past that laundromat so many times as it's close to his house and his studio. He wanted to shoot something there, and it ended up working out so well. I thought that was an amazing visual with the silhouette and all the colors, especially for the ending scene. I'm glad that he chose that.

RYAN CALAVANO, DIRECTOR:

That one shot was the thing I had in my head the whole time. Early on, I got a couple suggestions from friends to cut away quicker. I'm like "I'm going to trust my audience here that they're going to appreciate this beautiful shot. Let it be there for a little bit."

In the last shot where Taylor is sitting next to Jason and she looks over, that whole interaction at the end was straight up Jason and Taylor being amazing. I was like, "I'm going to get this last shot. You guys sit there." The interaction they did on their own. First take. It was sort of serendipitous. We went to shoot one day and we have six hundred bucks and we have four locations. If it works, that's lucky. If you love it and it's good, which was the case for this, that's a lot of serendipitous things that had to happen. That was one of them.

When a video plays as well as "Brea," it's easy for the viewer to overlook the struggle of its creators. Often the struggle is based in the mechanics, long hours, and equipment costs for a video with little to no budget. Other times, the struggle is fatigue and physical pain.

RYAN CALAVANO, DIRECTOR:

Nowadays, not a lot of people get big budgets. I don't really like them necessarily. I try to add it to my selling point to get hired, like "This is what we did for six hundred bucks, this is what we did for a thousand. We're doing legit things for nothing so if you gave us 10 grand, we could do crazy things.

None of us who are at this level doing indie music videos are doing it for the money. We want to be artists just like the musicians.

TAYLOR SWANTEK, DANCER:

For sure, it's not ideal. It's never an ideal situation to dance on concrete, especially with ballet. It's not a forgiving floor. Ryan and I talked about that ahead of time, and he wanted to make sure I was okay with that. I definitely wouldn't do it often, but for this video it was really important that we were outside in those locations. I tried to do a combination of certain technical moves that I wanted to show, but also play it safe in the sense that I wasn't going to be doing jetés[40] or jumping all day, because it would be really tough on my body. I would be asking for an injury if I tried to do that 30 times on uneven concrete, so instead I did a few leaps here, and different things there. My pointe shoes were pretty destroyed by the end of the day, which is not unusual for being on that kind of surface, but it worked out during filming. It went well overall and wasn't too much of an issue. The thing that worked in my favor is that we set it to be mostly improvised and not strict choreography. So that allowed me to work with whatever surface we were on. For example, the part down by the Riverwalk, there was a railing there that was like a ballet barre. It was perfect to play with and do something different, versus when we were in the underpass dancing around each other.

RYAN CALAVANO, DIRECTOR:

Everyone understood everything I was aiming for, from what I could glean from the YouTube comments. I just wanted to make something beautiful with a simple concept, and I really wanted to work with dancers. This is my first foray into something with dancers legitimately. A lot of people construed it in a way that was a little deeper than even what I got which I thought was cool.

TAYLOR SWANTEK, DANCER:

Yes, Ryan told me that part from the beginning, that that was his vision. I knew ahead of time that I was going to be his spirit and his soul in a sense. In addition to that, we definitely had some arcs within the story - different emotions that Jason was going to be feeling, certain ups and downs. The moment where someone's coming out of the store and he's reaching out asking for change, Ryan said, "Taylor, I want you to be near him, but then take your reaction of how it feels even further than what Jason's showing. So it shows the depth of how that rejection would feel which someone's not necessarily going to display outwardly. But that's really how it feels inside when it's the tenth time that's happened to you. So that you're going to kind of collapse to the floor." He gave us clear direction in certain scenes, in different moments, and then a lot of the connections we would fill in and play off of each other. We would start with one thing and try something else.

40 Definition of jeté: "Thrown. A jump from one foot to the other in which the working leg is brushed into the air and appears to be thrown. (zhuhTAY)"

RYAN CALAVANO, DIRECTOR:

Actually, I don't like sticking to lyrics of songs. I like to make supplementary concepts. That's why I like Open Mike Eagle so much. I'll come at him with a wild-ass concept and he'll be like, "Sure!" People will be like, "It has nothing to do with the song" and I'm like, "Now it does!"

RYAN CALAVANO, DIRECTOR:

If you noticed, there's no drone footage for this because I crashed it when we were down by the water. It hit the overpass and fell right in the water. I lost my drone. That's a funny little story.

TAYLOR SWANTEK, DANCER:

Ryan also had a drone that he was trying to take some aerial shots with, especially during the Riverwalk part. It was pretty windy and I remember Ryan was flying the drone around. We really couldn't hear because the drone was so loud. We were getting into the scene, and all of a sudden, the wind picked up and the drone got swept into the water. It was like, "Oh no!" But also the way it happened was pretty funny, and we all burst into laughter. I think the video turned out just fine without the aerial shots, so maybe it was meant to be.

RYAN CALAVANO, DIRECTOR:

That shoot was like we tried to cram so much stuff in there. It came out, so I have no complaints at all.

TAYLOR SWANTEK, DANCER:

This is one of my favorite things I've done my entire career.[41] I had such a great experience getting to work on this; getting to tell this beautifully poignant story, and have creative freedom. Ryan, Jason, and Sean were amazing, such a great team. I'm always going to have fond memories of the shoot. Watching it again before we had this interview, it felt like, "Aww." I'm proud of what we created. It's been really lovely to see a lot of positive responses to this video, too, and hearing how people interpret it in different ways.

---

41 This praise wouldn't mean as much coming from a less established dancer. Swantek has appeared in major videos including Johnny Yukon's "Lonely," Vice's "Steady 1234," Kygo's "Stole the Show," and Taylor Swift's "Shake It Off." At the time of writing, those videos have roughly the following views: 210,000, 270,000, 340,000,000, and 2,900,000,000. Those last two would read "three hundred forty million" and "two point nine billion" by the way!

COUSINS

L'ORANGE: ALONE

XZIBIT: WHAT U SEE IS WHAT U GET

ODDISEE: TINY DESK CONCERT

THE WISDOM OF ODDISEE

At times, listening to Oddisee feels like reading a sacred religious text or some lost Paolo Coelho novel. His song concepts are rooted in the most important tenets of life- hope, struggle, confusion. While other rappers tackle the philosophy of life, Oddisee's lyrics often read differently- less like a current rap song and more like the aforementioned religious or inspirational text. I wondered if people could tell the difference. I created a quiz where the subject had to decide whether the text selection was from an Oddisee song or an inspirational poem.

1. If you can keep your head when all about you
   Are losing theirs and blaming it on you
   If you can trust yourself when all men doubt you
   But make allowance for their doubting too

2. The tree that never had to fight
   For sun and sky and air and light
   But stood out in the open plain
   And always got its share of rain

3. Living in the moment got a hopeless feel
   But the feeling in itself got its own appeal
   I know, I'm attracted to the lights in the distance
   The closer that I get and the brighter my wish gets
   Excited by the risk and the chances I'm taking
   Not sure what I'm putting my faith in

4. Figure it out for yourself, my lad,
   You've all the greatest of men have had
   Two arms, two hands, two legs, two eyes
   And a brain to use if you would be wise.

5. You may write me down in history
With your bitter, twisted lies
You may tread me in the very dirt
But still, like dust, I rise

6. When you told me the truth even if it really hurt
'Cause you knew a lie was worse
That's love
When you let me borrow money that you really didn't have
'Cause you knew what I was worth
That's love

7. I'm just trying to break out the mold
Trying to do the opposite of everything that I'm told
Try to put me in a box, already in a globe
So I don't get offended by the thinking of the old

8. I've spent some time alone
I'm looking forward, don't want to be found but I'm a going
And keep searching on it, it's out there so I explore it
But when I chose to ignore it, that's of course when I found it
When I stopped looking

Answers: 1) *If* by Rudyard Kipling 2) *Good Timber* by Douglas Malloch 3) *Own Appeal* by Oddisee 4) *Equipment* by Edgar Guest 5) *Still I Rise* by Maya Angelou 6) *That's Love* by Oddisee 7) *Belong to the World* by Oddisee 8) *When I Stopped Looking* by Markis Precise f/ Oddisee

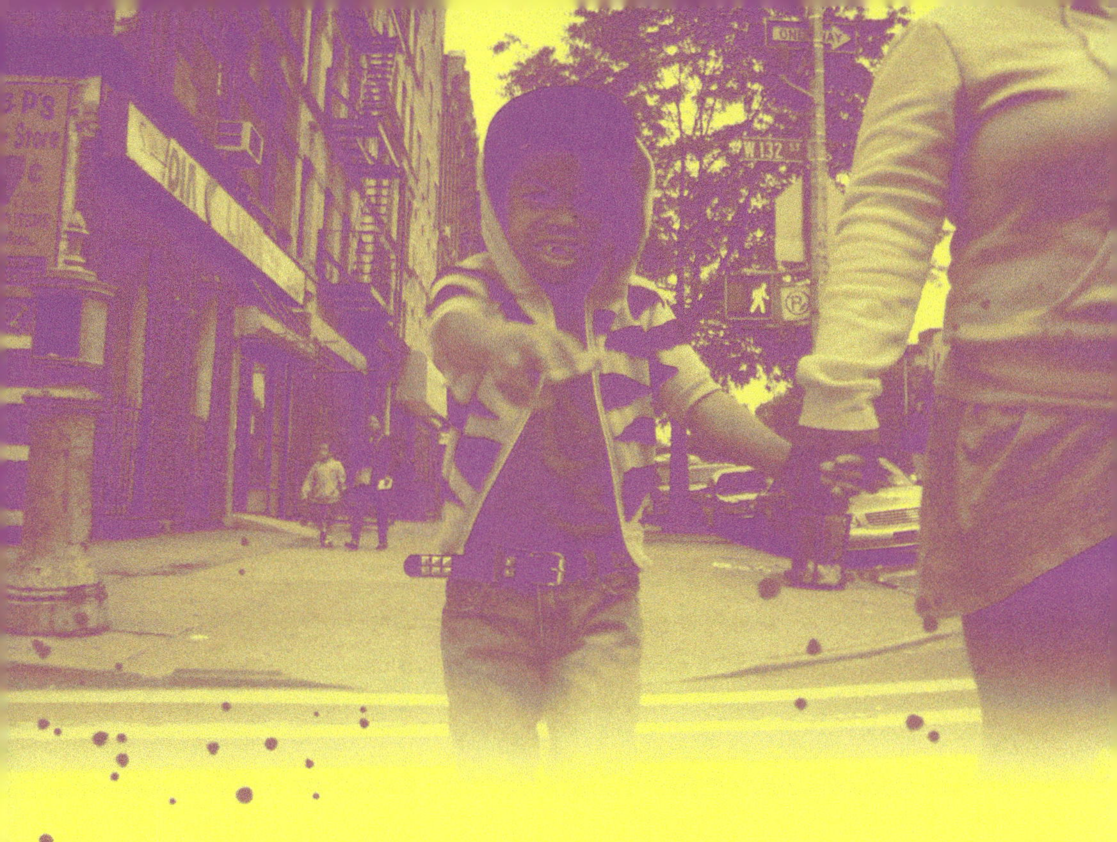

CHAPTER 5

DANNY BROWN: GROWN UP

GREG BRUNKALLA, DIRECTOR:

It's interesting that you're talking about this because as you were calling me, I was texting Dave[42] from Chromeo. He was a big part of this. Dave is brothers with A-Trak[43] who owns Fool's Gold[44] and has a band called Chromeo. They're doing really well. When I moved to New York in 2001, Chromeo was just playing little gigs in New York. They're from Montreal. I did some stuff for Chromeo. I was out one night and I ran into Dave and A-Trak at a restaurant in Williamsburg. I was just like, "If you guys ever need videos, let me know." A-Trak was like, "We might have something. You should stop by the office." They had an office on Metropolitan.[45] I stopped over there. They have this track. Scion's going to pay for it, not a lot of money. Like $5,000. I was just like "I'll put my own resources into it." They were like, "It's about growing up, so maybe there's a kid in it." And that was it. I wrote a bunch of different ideas. That's sort of how it came about. It's funny talking about it, because I just reached out to Dave about a week or so ago, like "If you need any videos I'm ready to do another one."

Before I did that video and ever talked to A-Trak, I always wanted to do a Danny Brown video. That was always on my radar. He just seems like a different kind of rapper. I want to be associated with people who do different shit. That's a funny story I guess.

This was a two-day shoot. The video I shot in Brooklyn and Harlem. I shot it right outside my apartment in Williamsburg, where I am right now. I shot it around here and then I shot it up in Harlem. We got a school in Harlem to let us use their school for location. While we were up there,

---

42 David "Dave 1" Macklovitch.

43 A-Trak was the first DJ to win all three major DJ competitions. He and Dave 1 were members of the collective Obscure Disorder. You can witness his skills on the excellent "2004." Oh, he also served as Kanye West's tour DJ.

44 Fool's Gold Records, founded by A-Trak and Nick Catchdubs, is the home to many acts, including BROCKHAMPTON, Chromeo, Cool Kids, Danny Brown, Duck Sauce, Kid Cudi, Lil D, LNDN DRGS, Meyhem Lauren, Party Supplies, and Run The Jewels.

45 Metropolitan Avenue runs roughly 8 miles through Queens and Brooklyn, from the East River in Williamsburg to Jamaica, Queens.

kind of behind the Apollo Theater[46]. That's where we shot the final scene, where he's walking and he turns into Danny Brown. A funny story about that one actually. They[47] said, "Just put a kid in it." I said, "I actually want to put Danny Brown in it too." They were like, "He lives in Detroit." I said "Yeah, well just fly him in." They were like, "What do you need him to do?" I was like, "I need him for the last shot. I want the kid to turn into him." "For one shot you want us to fly him in?" I'm like, "Do you want to fly him in for 80 shots or just one? It will be easy for him. It will validate it. It won't look like someone [unofficial] made it. It will make it official." I really, really pushed for it. It was one of those things I was really, really pushing for, but at the same time questioning myself. Man, I'm really taking Danny Brown, telling him to get on a plane. I don't know this guy and I'm making him come to Harlem for one shot. To me, he was like the punctuation. It was the fun. I like to give videos and stories a reason to watch them to the very end. Also, when I talk to people, then I know if they've watched the whole thing or not.

I didn't want the fan-made video vibe. It definitely sealed the deal on that. I think it's fair game though. If someone makes a good video, it's a good video. And if the label signs off on it, it's fair game.

MICHAEL BELCHER, CINEMATOGRAPHER:

It's been awhile since [Greg and I] worked together. Maybe three years. I've been meaning to try to reconnect with him. He is a super terrific, talented guy.

I met him on the job a few years before that. It might have been five years before I was shooting, I was just like a driver. I was the driver/runner/utility person for him for a job at Bonnaroo. The DP was Scott Sans. I met those guys at the same time, and they became long-term collaborators for several years. Scott was DP, Greg was director and I was like the driver. I did a number of jobs with him in that role, and I did a bunch of travel jobs with Scott Sands as his AC[48]. I'd shoot a second camera. Sometimes, he was doing TV shows for Sharp entertainment. He does a bunch of Andrew Zimmern shows. There's a bunch of eating shows. He did a show with a guy named Bert Kreischer. He's a comedian who is going around doing a lot of live feeds at theme parks.[49] I went

46 The school was most likely Democracy Prep Endurance Charter School.

47 Fools Gold.

48 Assistant Camera.

49 Bert the Conqueror

all around the country for months and months doing that. It was a landmark for me and my career with starting to shoot at that time. Scott was trying to translate into being a Steadicam operator instead of being DP. When Greg had the idea to do all the Steadicam work, Scott was like, "Great, but I just want to focus on Steadicam. Why don't we give the DP role to Mike?" That's how it came to be. Scott just kind of handed it over to me so he could focus on Steadicam. At that time, he was sort of just practicing. Now, he's a full fledged union Steadicam operator who's doing shows and commercials. So, yeah, I kind of started with them as a driver and they were kind enough to give me the opportunity. It was years later, but just thinking about that evolution is really important to me.

MELISSA VARGAS, COSTUME DESIGN:

Greg is amazing at giving direction. He's one of my favorite directors. We still work together. I love him so much.

DANTE HOAGLAND, ACTOR, PLAYING LIL' DANNY BROWN:[50]

My name is Dante Hoagland and I'm 9 years old. This is my first video I ever did. When I grow up, my "always dream" was to go to California to see what Hollywood was and go on Disney and Nickelodeon shows. Don't ever say you can't do nothing. You can do it. Just try.

GREG BRUNKALLA, DIRECTOR, "GROWN UP":

I don't remember, but I just know that the audition was sort of short notice. We didn't have much money either. Normally, when I shoot a video or a commercial, you see like 400-500 people. We needed a lot of cast, but I say for every person we cast, we see like 50 people. The day before, with such specific needs, an African American kid with an attitude. There's not a lot. Maybe 15 kids came in. Not a lot. I don't think he saw any (video) clips of Danny. Maybe he did his research. I don't think so.

DANTE HOAGLAND, ACTOR, PLAYING LIL' DANNY BROWN:

First, I had to audition, which was pretty easy. The night before that, me and my mom were studying, practicing the song, and when I did the audition it felt good.

---

50 I was unable to interview Dante for this piece. At the time of writing, he stars on the Tracy Morgan vehicle "The Last O.G." Dante's quotes are taken from "Danny Brown - Behind-the-scenes @ "Grown Up" Video Shoot (Scion AV), hosted at https://www.youtube.com/watch?v=bfxgT1aVaic.

Brunkalla, who was unable to handle the casting process himself, was told that casting revealed a clear winner. You can actually watch Hoagland's audition on YouTube, as he raps and dances along to Drake's "The Motto" and Danny Brown's "Grown Up."[51]

GREG BRUNKALLA, DIRECTOR, "GROWN UP."

No, that's the casting director.[52] I can't remember where I was at the time. I don't know if I was in New York at the time. I feel like I was on a job or something. The casting house that I always use, House Casting actually, asked kids to come in and sing. They got the track the day before. Just come in and sing something you know just to show me what that looks like. If you can sing the song, great. If you can't, you can just bring something you know so I know what it looks like when you can perform something. They came in at the end of the day. The casting director would usually say "you should check out these few people." He was pretty much like, "You really just need to check out one guy. I think we found him. He's amazing." He did the actual song word for word. He had the song under 24 hours. I looked at some of the others and one kid brought in Barney. Someone sang a kids' song that they knew, which was fair enough. Dante just came in and nailed it. He's *the video.* If it wasn't for him... Casting is so important. The crazy thing is that you probably don't know: Right around when I was making the video, when I was storyboarding it and location scouting and coming up with everything, my friend said, "Hey, you've got to see this. Some kid is rapping a Kanye West song and it's going viral." She shows me this video of this kid in Manhattan. A little black kid, who doesn't really look like Kanye West but he's rapping a Kanye West song. Nobody knows about it now but at the time, for like a week, this thing was being sent around. What happens a lot when you're doing creative work, [is that] you see something that's similar to what [you're] trying to do. They were cutting a lot because he couldn't sing it. They were cutting around where he would mess up. There were so many edits. So I watched that and I was like, "You know what? I got to do long takes. I got to do takes where we're not editing." I mean we'll edit between scenes. But we're really not editing within a scene. So when he's walking across the street holding his mom's hand, there's no cuts. It cuts to the next scene. It's helpful to see the (YouTube) video[53] and think, "Why am I not impressed?"

---

51 Dante Hoagland audition for Danny Brown - Grown Up music video. https://www.youtube.com/watch?v=D-klol66lbSo

52 Speaking with Dante Hoagland in the video, "Danny Brown - Behind-the-scenes @ "Grown Up" Video Shoot (Scion AV), hosted at https://www.youtube.com/watch?v=bfxgT1aVaic.

53 The video of the kid rapping Kanye.

GREG BRUNKALLA, DIRECTOR, "GROWN UP:"

Spike Jonze did a kid rapping video back in the day with Biggie and Puffy.[54] I love Spike, but the last thing I want to do is rip anyone off. I mean the song is called "Grown Up." It's about him as a kid. That's the concept. I'm not going to fight that at all. The label sort of suggested it. Maybe if the kid Fool's Gold. I just wrote the story around it. Obviously casting is going to be so key. He's just a kid but he's really gotta nail it.

MELISSA VARGAS, COSTUME DESIGN:

Dante is like the happiest kid in the world, so getting him to act mad... [Greg] kept asking [Dante] to be a little more angry or mad for certain lyrics, to act tougher. But Dante has a huge smile on his face. After every take of acting mad, he has a big smile on his face asking "Is that okay?" There's a lot of curses in the raps in the lyrics. [Dante's mother] was like, "He knows that he's acting. But in real life, we don't get these words. We don't use this language." It was very cool to see how she was teaching him that that was bad language. He's an incredible actor so she was making sure he could differentiate those two things which I thought was great.

DANTE HOAGLAND, ACTOR, PLAYING LIL' DANNY BROWN:

When I met Danny Brown, he said "How you doing?" I was like, "Good."

MICHAEL BELCHER, CINEMATOGRAPHER:

He didn't meet Danny Brown until we had that second shoot day, basically for that last shot. He saw the way that Danny always stuck his tongue out and made these crazy faces. Every single shot he did after that, he totally incorporated that. He really got it. No one told him that. He saw Danny Brown and then layered on what he picked up from him. Like any pro would do. Up until [Dante] met [Danny,] a lot of what he was doing was more classic, hip-hop, physical motions with the verses. But when he met him, he got very specific with the tongue out. Things he hadn't done up to that point.

MICHAEL BELCHER, CINEMATOGRAPHER:

That was sort of early in my career as a DP. The real trick with that one was more technical. Some videos have these sort of categories of commercial video and narrative. Sometimes, they

---

54 Notorious B.I.G. "Sky's the Limit"

feel distinctly in one category, and sometimes they overlap. Some videos are like short films and there are films that feel like music videos. So this particular music video was a pretty traditional music video where they're focused on being interesting visually and not necessarily creating a whole lot of meaning. There wasn't a whole lot of emotional preparation, so more a lot of technical preparation. Like, "How do we make this concept of constantly moving Steadicam with this little boy? How do we make that interesting?" It was a matter of saying that a lot of the shots are going to be him walking towards the camera. "How do we time that out, shot by shot?" So it's a little more like doing math. "Where are the interesting locations? What actions might he do? How do we time them out to fit into the song in the right way?" It's a very technical thing to measure those things out. To be there with Greg and Scott and say, "How much time will it take to get from the start of the shot to the end? What word will he start on? What word will he end on?" Then, creating a meaning based on that environment and the props. Or his wardrobe might have something to do with that particular line of the song. And create meaning in that way. But it's largely technical. In that case, some jobs are just kind of like doing math and trying to make sure everything technically is going to be cohesive and tight. Other jobs of course require a more soulful approach. How should this feel based on this moment. If I walk into this room and look through the lens, how does that feel? Does it feel appropriate? Either supporting or in some way subverting the thing you're actually shooting. So those more emotional scenes and more emotional projects, it's kind of a different side of the brain.

GREG BRUNKALLA, DIRECTOR, "GROWN UP."

I wasn't really like that as a kid honestly. It was kind of just inspired by living in New York, and thinking, "What can you do in the park? What's already there? He can push over a garbage can. And then in a clothing store." I'm actually about to walk by a lot of these locations. The clothing store is right by my apartment. Outside the clothing store, it's like the little slide that he's on. The thing you put your quarter in. That's right there. Where he crashes his bike is about one block from my apartment. Where he squirts the gun, that's the next street over. We did most of the shots around there the one day. The bike accident we figured out. I was kind of inspired by location. You can walk into any location and be like, "What would a kid do in here to cause trouble?" That's kind of it.

We put stuff on there. We probably put a piece of plexi on there. He's singing about making girls wet or something like that. So that's why. Everything kind of has a reason. If we use a squirt gun, it seems kind of innocent.

It was [a charter school.] They didn't ask us for much money. It's hard. New York Public Schools don't let you shoot in them. So we wanted that public school vibe.

DANTE HOAGLAND, ACTOR, PLAYING LIL' DANNY BROWN:

The favorite part of my video was the library. I was throwing all the books around.

GREG BRUNKALLA, DIRECTOR, "GROWN UP":

Who gets pelted with TP? I don't remember. That was a member of our crew. My nickname is Brunx. That is written in the bathroom. He kicks the door open and it says Danny Brown on the door. And then it says Brunx somewhere in the bathroom. I do that with a lot of my videos. I'll tag 'Brunx' somewhere.

DANTE HOAGLAND, ACTOR, PLAYING LIL' DANNY BROWN:

The hardest thing was when they were swinging me around, my hands were hurting but I toughed it out. And when I finally got off, I was dizzy.

MICHAEL BELCHER, CINEMATOGRAPHER:

There's this other brief moment where Dante's flying. He's being held by his hands and whisked around in the circle like a merry-go-round. Scott Sands, he's a strong person. I was like, 'Scott I think we can do this if you hold him, twirling around and I just jump on your back, wrap my legs around your waist, I hold the camera right next to your ear so it's kind of like pointing down from just beside your head. If you just spin around holding me on top of you, then I think it will work. It's just an example of an extremely lo-fi thing. Literally, I'm basically getting a piggyback ride from him and he's holding this little boy and spinning him at the same time. And I have the camera pressed against his head and pointed at the boy. The gaffer, Danny April, he took a video of that, which I probably have somewhere. It's kind of funny because it just looks like we're messing on the playground or something. From the perspective of the lens, it got us that little moment in a pretty unique way. I've never really seen that done before in that way. It was again just another thing that we wanted to do and try to figure out. Just thought of a solution, went for it, and it worked.

GREG BRUNKALLA, DIRECTOR, "GROWN UP:"

That was a rigging. That was super lo-fi. We might have a picture of that somewhere. My cinematographer Michael Belcher was spinning around, and I think somebody was holding him.

I can't remember exactly, it was really weird. It was super Lo-Fi.

Outside of the spinning scene, one other scene was most difficult to capture.

MICHAEL BELCHER, CINEMATOGRAPHER:

There are two shots that come to mind. One is when he wrecks his bike. He's in slow motion flying towards us. Scott and Greg were working on that and I was around the corner looking at the next shot or something. I came over and they were trying to figure it out. It just really occurred to me how to do it as soon as I saw everything laid out. The way we ended up doing it was, in order to get him sort of flying toward the camera in slow motion, we actually needed to have his weight on something. We couldn't just throw him. We had to support him almost like a diving board under his shirt. We were trying to figure it out and this video was made for like zero money. None of us got paid. I think it might have been $5,000 all in. I think that just went towards food and gas. No one got paid. Almost all the gear was donated by people who owned it. We had no grip gear to make the build. So Leah, the producer, actually put her arm underneath Dante's shirt. You couldn't see her hand and she just sort of held him up and sort of moved him towards the camera. He just acted like he was flying towards us. It's a super duper lo-fi thing. It's very simple because in the shot he's just kind of moving a little bit but there is no other way to get it in the moment. We just did it. As soon as I had the idea, we had the shot in five minutes. Just an odd solution because we didn't have anything else.

So much of it was really found on the fly. I just think that this boy just brought it. No matter what we were doing, he seemed to know more than anybody about the song. How to do it. It was like having a real proper actor there who is over-prepared and knew everything. And we put the camera on them and was just like, "Wow, this is great." He brought it in such an amazing way. It's funny. The shot of him holding the lady's hand. That's actually his mom when he is crossing the street there.

It's beautiful because this whole thing is just him and his mom. His mom's the one who's pushing them in that cart down the street. There's just a handful of people there. There's no wasted motion. We had them two days of shooting and both days we had amazing AC's.

GREG BRUNKALLA, DIRECTOR, "GROWN UP:"

That was my wardrobe stylist. Her name's Melissa Vargas. I think that was her first solo gig actually as a stylist. She nailed it. I had never met her before. I told her, "This is what I need done," and she nailed it. Now we've worked together a ton. She's doing movies now. I just shot a short film I've been working on for a while and she wasn't even available to help me on that (laughing). She's super loyal. We're all super loyal when we work on these things together. We all sort of came up together. Yeah Melissa Vargas. Check her out.

MICHAEL BELCHER, CINEMATOGRAPHER:

Melissa, the wardrobe designer was great. She made that sweatshirt, that tiger sweatshirt. That's actually a hooded sweatshirt made for a dog. Super ingenious. She's a real talent. She's amazing at her job. That was such a breakthrough because at that time, Danny Brown had been known to wear that type of sweatshirt. She just created this mini version. I don't even know how she came to the point of finding one made for a dog. I'm sure she went to American Apparel and happened to find it. It's actually really cool. A short sleeve hoodie? Killer.

MELISSA VARGAS, COSTUME DESIGN:

I think at the time, he was known for his eclectic style, for sure. I think in the hip hop scene it was a bit controversial. As I'm sure you know, he was going to sign with G-Unit and they asked him to change his appearance.[55] He declined and then ended up going with ASAP Rocky's label, if I'm not mistaken. So what I usually do when I have a project, and after discussing with Greg, I started doing a lot of research on him and what he wears to perform. I looked at a lot of images that were out there. It wasn't traditional streetwear that a rapper would wear, so I tried to find the same thing with kids clothes. One problem that I came up against was that the kids clothes were not fitted enough for the actor we were using. I had to go two sizes smaller so his jeans could be tighter, so everything was very fitted. He was a very small kid. I think we were getting clothes for a 5 year old.

MICHAEL BELCHER, CINEMATOGRAPHER:

As soon as I saw the kid doing work and the wardrobe coming together and the Steadicam shots really fitting, I was like, "Okay this thing has a real opportunity."

55 Rob Markman quotes Danny at http://www.mtv.com/news/1669170/danny-brown-xxx-mixtape/: "It was a real thing. 50 was with it; he just didn't sign me because of my jeans. He liked the music, but he didn't like the way I looked."

MELISSA VARGAS, COSTUME DESIGN:

Dante really wanted the denim vest that was embroidered on the back. He had a lot of photos of him wearing that cut off denim vest with a t-shirt. It was a great idea to do the opening credits of the music video on the back of the jacket. It was great. He was really, really excited when we gave him the denim jacket because he was going to wear it to school the next day.

During the prep of the music video, Greg wanted to replicate the hoodie. It needed to be really fast, so I was trying to desperately find an orange hoodie that we could convert. But I couldn't find a hoodie anywhere that matched that color it was. American Apparel was still open, so I went to American Apparel. I was basically begging them to look for an orange hoodie, when behind the counter I see this orange hoodie. I was like "What is that? For babies?" They were like, "No, it's a dog hoodie," and I was like "What is the biggest size that comes in?" I was so excited. Then I took it home, I cut out.... This was a very low budget music video, so we were making everything ourselves. I got black fabric and I cut out the tiger stripes, hand stitched them myself, and then prayed that it would work. But I didn't get to see the actor the day before. We tried it on on the set and it fit perfectly on the actor. We were able to replicate that look and I think that was such a specific look for him at the time. He was doing so many performances with that jacket. It was an Adidas custom-made jacket. He was touring. There are so many images of him. Being able to replicate that was a big deal. I feel like we needed it. That's what stood out the most in the music video, because it was like this mini version is really wearing a dog sweatshirt that I found by chance.

I don't know what happened to the hoodie. I handed it over to production. The production company owns all that stuff. It was a mix of his clothes and clothes that I had purchased for him. We had to incorporate Dante's wardrobe. We asked his mom to bring a bunch of his clothes to the set. The leather jacket was his. I had a couple different hats for him.

DANTE HOAGLAND, ACTOR, PLAYING LIL' DANNY BROWN:

He had to put a wig in my hair. It was fun.

MELISSA VARGAS, COSTUME DESIGN:

It was pretty great. For some reason, I was also in charge of hair. We didn't have a hair person. We had this wig that I had cut up that I pinned in Dante's hair so it could look like Danny Brown's bangs. I had the chipped tooth that we would paint over his tooth in the scene after he got into the bicycle accident.

DANTE HOAGLAND, ACTOR, PLAYING LIL' DANNY BROWN:

When we saw the video, the funniest thing was when I fell off my bike. It was this hole inside the ground and there they're picking me up by the bike like I was falling, and I made that facial expression. It was funny. They put gum in there. It was coloring like candy color it tasted good. It was like, minty. They had to make me look like Danny Brown when he was a little kid. They had to paint my tooth black.

MELISSA VARGAS, COSTUME DESIGN:

It was a beard that I found. I have a bunch of random things, costumes that I collect that I'm just like "I'll find a use for that." [Remembering] It *was* a beard. I was like, "This could work." We were very, very lucky with a lot of things.

GREG BRUNKALLA, DIRECTOR, "GROWN UP:"

When he's riding that toy, we weren't sure of the order we were shooting in. He actually has his broken tooth on. So I had him rap the whole song on there. We put the edit together, I'm like "Shit! He has a broken tooth." So in post, they put his tooth back on. Then there's another shot where it's the opposite. I think when he's spinning. I think they put the chip back on his tooth because I fucked up. Those are the little things that we would let slide back in the day. But I won't let that shit slide anymore.[56] I'm going to beg for somebody to put his tooth back on. Because there's a little bit of a story there when he breaks his tooth.

GREG BRUNKALLA, DIRECTOR, "GROWN UP:"

I just remember when Danny Brown finally got there, we're shooting in Harlem. You know that piece of wood on the side? We shot on this janky street that was all boarded up. I couldn't find Danny Brown, but I could smell weed. He was hiding from Dante. He crawled under there and was smoking weed underneath the board. I was like, "What's up man?" I'm back there in the shitty lot talking to Danny Brown trying to get him pumped up. He's got the best attitude. He just laughs about everything. He's the nicest guy.

---

56 Out of all the quotes I have received for this book, this one is the line that most reads like an inspirational Run The Jewels lyric.

COUSINS

NOTORIOUS B.I.G.: SKY'S THE LIMIT

88 KEYS + KANYE WEST: STAY UP (VIAGRA)

THE AVALANCHES: BECAUSE I'M ME

THE STRUGGLE

Working behind the scenes on a music video is not what most would expect. Budgets are typically small or non-existent. The video's creators rely on their friends and industry connects to acquire free or discounted services. Many creators work day (or night) jobs and support musical artists in their free time, hoping to create something meaningful or bolster their portfolios. My discussions with Michael, Melissa, and Greg and many other interviews inspired the title for this book, *For The Love.*

While interviewing, transcribing, compiling, and editing this book, I felt a tight kinship with my interviewees. While I did have dreams that *FTL* could perhaps pay for a burrito or pair of sneakers or a used car, my real motivation was to document an important part of hip-hop history; to repay a debt to a culture that has given me so much. Some stories from my interviewees:

Melissa Vargas, Costume Design: I had very little sleep. I was a bit delirious because I had another job at a bar at the time. I think I maybe got an hour of sleep when we shot it and did the whole shoot.

Michael Belcher, Cinematographer: It's really interesting. So often we do jobs that are small in size. For whatever reason, it happens fairly often that some of the best work that we get to be a part of is non-paying, most free creatively. This is no exception. It's hard to tell what's going to hit. When I look at my website, the stuff I've kept on there as my curated presentation, a lot of that is totally non-paying or barely paying. But the opportunity was different or more free. It's a good reminder that, big or small, the opportunities are everything. It's kind of hard to predict what's really going to hit.

Those things get back to you though. The fact that I shot that I'm sure has gotten me other work, in the sense that people liked it. It's always about the long game. No matter what I'm working on, whether I'm getting paid properly or not, "Will this matter a year from now?'

That's always something I'm coming back to. Every job is a risk in that way but in terms of pushing hard and doing everything you can, it's that long view.

It's always hard. If it's a job worth doing, it's going to suck at some point. If you don't get to the point that's like, "Why am I doing this? I should have said no. I should have become a barber." If you don't reach that point, you're probably repeating yourself and that's not quite challenging enough. That pain and suffering is the signpost of something valuable.

Greg Brunkalla, Director, "Grown Up:" If you knew how many music videos I've written for how many I've shot. It makes me sick to my stomach. I don't do a lot because they're exhausting.

There's a story there for sure man. If you saw the folder of treatments I have. To be able to sit down. If you've talked to 50 people, maybe it's a broken record, but sit down with a blank paper and have that enthusiasm after you just you've done it over and over. It takes a lot of psychological warfare on yourself. I'm curious what you've heard.

I think of it like photographers doing a cover. Like doing an editorial. My photographer friends. They'll get enough money to do it. But they don't really walk away with anything. It's sort of the same thing. I think the annoying thing is when people treat you like they're giving you this privilege or opportunity because they don't know how much goes into it. I cash in all my favors. I do a lot of commercials. I go to The Mill, which is one of the best effects houses. I have great cinematographers and Steadicam operators. And AD's. The whole nine. You do a music video and people are like giving you hell about stuff. I have to bite my tongue sometimes. Like, man if you knew how many favors I'm pulling and how many people I have to stroke, not physically, to get this to happen. I don't know if you saw my video for The Avalanches? The shoot in the subway cost a lot of money. It was half the budget. I had to meet the MTA. I had to go to the MTA, present my idea to them, play the song, basically act it out. Because there's not a lot of money and they don't want to work on a Sunday. They're like, "What is this thing that you want to bother us about?" It's that kind of attitude. I don't want to sound bitter, but it's a lot more work than just "action."

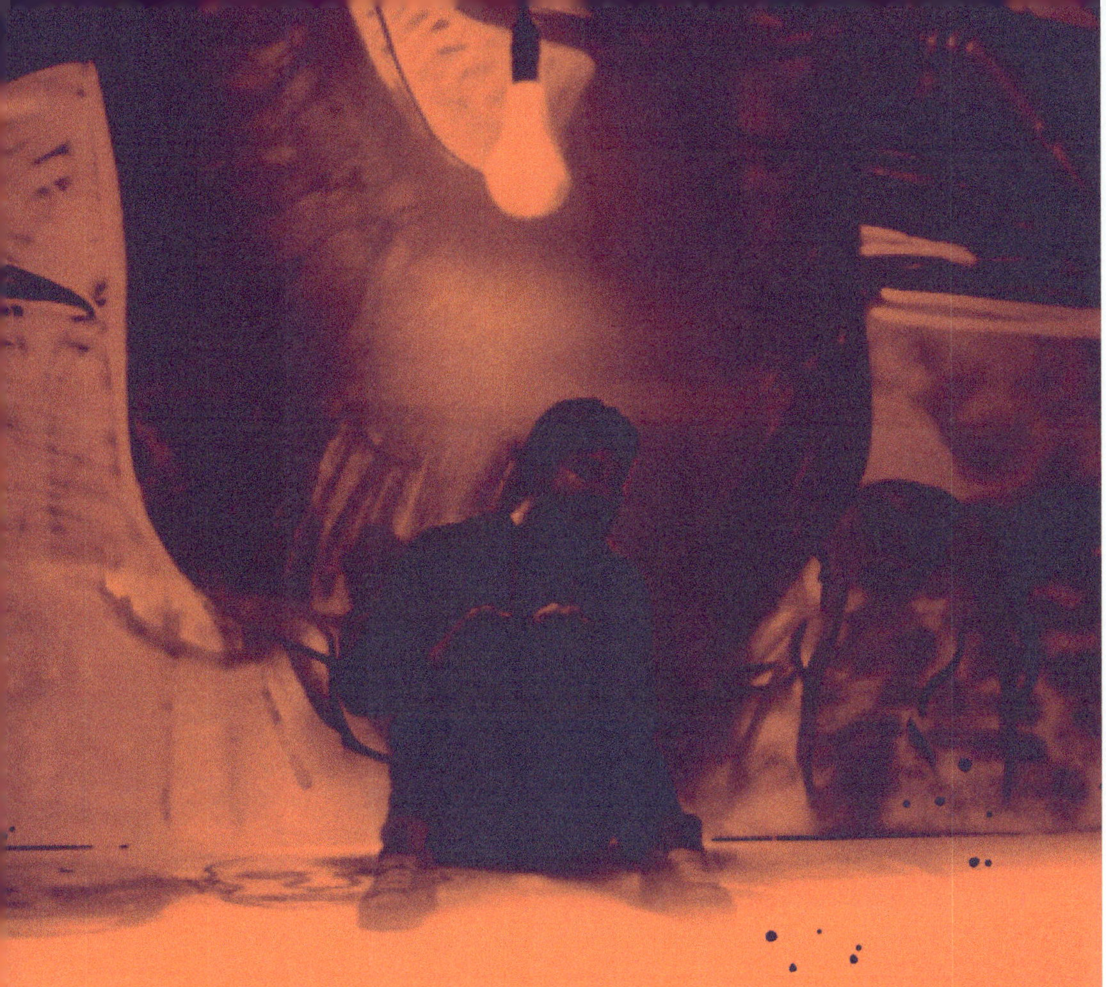

CHAPTER 6

AESOP ROCK:
ZERO DARK THIRTY

ISAAC RAVISHANKARA, DIRECTOR, "ZERO DARK THIRTY:"

This one was funny because around the time I pitched on the Atmosphere one[57], I might have pitched on another Aesop Rock video. All the people I grew up with were listening to hip-hop. Atmosphere was hugely important but Aesop was the top! I grew up with the 3Oh3![58] kids, especially Sean[59], the guy who writes the lyrics for that band. He was just a crazy underground hip-hop head. He introduced me to a lot of this stuff. Rhymesayers stuff, Cannibal Ox stuff. I still believe there is no one who's been lyrically similar to Aesop Rock. He's the best. You could spend weeks dissecting the lyrics. He was always a big part of what I listened to. They came back around and said, "Hey, this is a project that we want to do. Would Isaac be interested?" I immediately told my rep "Yes! No matter what." And they're like. "Okay, cool but we have to put it out in two weeks and we have no money." I was like, "I don't care. It's cool. We'll do it." So that was how it came up. They had the song. I think they had maybe gone down the road of doing something else for the video and it had fallen apart.

ISAAC RAVISHANKARA, DIRECTOR, "ZERO DARK THIRTY:"

He is a really awesome guy, but kind of hard to follow sometimes. He's very specific. I think they had gotten to the point where they were like, "We just need you to do something." So he and I got on a call and I remember it was like midnight one night. I said "All right, cool, let's just brainstorm until we get somewhere." He had that artist friend, CORO, who he was really eager about doing something with. Both of them were living up in the Bay at the time. The initial idea right off the bat was it would be really cool to not try to do anything super narrative but just to have... he said, "I have this idea to just be in a room rapping, and CORO would just be painting in the room." That was the initial idea, and it felt more like an old school hip hop video; two of the pillars of hip-hop[60] happening at the same time. We worked it out from there. Again, I had been paying attention

---

57 Isaac Ravishankara directed the Atmosphere video "The Last To Say." This will be covered in a future *For The Love* volume.

58 Boulder, CO electronic duo, who have worked with heavyweights like Katy Perry and Ke$ha.

59 Sean Foreman.

60 For my non hip-hop readers, the four pillars of hip-hop are generally considered to be DJing, emceeing, breakdancing, and graffiti.

to some time-lapse stuff and I had been monkeying around with time-lapse on the side for fun. This had come after the Atmosphere video and again, there's a lot of leverage to be had from no resources except for a static camera. Then, through brute strength, you can make something cool happen if the camera doesn't move. You don't have to have crazy skills or technology to composite two images together. So that kind of quickly turned into the idea of "What if he was rapping?" We initially thought we might do it with green screen. Like, "What if he's rapping and the painting is a time-lapse thing behind him?" We tried to talk about how long it would take to paint the piece. It would take a really long time and we just wanted it to be a little more dynamic. So that was sort of the next day. Like "alright cool, so what if there's you rapping and the painting is happening time-lapse behind it instead of in real time?" My initial idea was to do it with green screen. Then I talked to some guys I knew in LA about it. I realized that the green screen would be kind of hard to track the painting on to the wall. A friend of mine in LA who's good at effects stuff cooked up this idea that if he was against the white wall, you could use a white wall as basically a way of doing a green screen thing. You can just trace him because you can cut out everything that's white instead of everything that's green. Then, we could do that time-lapse on top of the white wall, and then you basically would put the two images together where you trace around Ian as he's rapping. And then, you have the time-lapse going secondary to that, because once you start painting the wall it stops being white. But then you have a bunch of footage with him against the white wall. In the same image, you have the wall being painted. This is day three at this point. I put together a really quick treatment and got back to him like, I think we can do this Everyone signed off on it. We decided right at that stage that it would be really cool to do not just one shot because it'll get really boring. We want to be able to cut different performances. We want to be able to do more than one performance. We need to be able to cut. We decided on a setup where we would shoot with 5 different cameras, all of which would not see the other ones and all of which would be locked off at different angles. And we would have a big white wall. We would shoot all the performance stuff first on one day where he's performing. Then you shoot all of the time-lapse of the wall being painted with all five of the cameras from a time-lapse. From camera one, you have images of him rapping and the wall being painted that you can composite. From camera two, three, four, and five.

CORO, ARTIST, "ZERO DARK THIRTY:"

The trick was all about having the fixed cameras. By having the fixed cameras at set points, you can film anything and lay it on top of each other.

That was what they would do too. If I remember correctly, they filmed the wall blank. then, filmed me painting it. They also had to film Ian over the blank wall rapping. I use it all of the time for photography stuff. Shooting double exposure. Shooting a couple of exposures, multiple exposures, and just overlaying them in Photoshop. Really easy way to get a complex scene. You don't have to arrange everything to get that right moment.

ISAAC RAVISHANKARA, DIRECTOR, "ZERO DARK THIRTY:"

So that became the plan. Myself and Kevin[61], my cinematographer, jumped on that. We jumped in a car and drove up to San Francisco to figure out where we were going to shoot this and how. Two days later, we had a warehouse space that we found in Oakland that we could shoot it at. The next day, we started shooting it. We shot all of the performance stuff the first night. We got in and set everything up, shot performance with Ian[62] for two hours or so the first night. The second day was a 12 or 14 hour day. We were just hanging out listening to music while Coro was painting.

CORO, ARTIST, "ZERO DARK THIRTY:"

We didn't walk into it with a set subject matter, if I remember correctly. They might have had a short list of things they wanted me to paint. By the end of it, it was kind of "Try this, try this!" It was a marathon day. We were in there all day. I won't lie, man. It was pretty hard dude. There was a lot of movement. I was sore for like a week. Just all of the getting up and running around. It's pretty physical painting like that. It was intense. It was a fun day though. I had a blast doing it.

CORO, ARTIST, "ZERO DARK THIRTY":

That wall was trashed by the end. Because there was so much paint so quickly that.... usually when you paint a mural, you're not going to re-paint it 30 times. This gallery out in Oakland lent us the space to do it in. We set up the wall. The guys came in and set up the cameras and shit. By the end of the day, if you stuck your finger in the way, your finger would go like a quarter inch into the wall. It was wet gooey paint. You could scratch into it and see the layers. It was a lot of paint. We blazed through a shit ton of paint that day. It was kind of a weird one, because I didn't get to make anything look really good. It was all rush-through, sketchy shit. It was interesting to use that much paint and at the end, end up with nothing for it. It was more the action of it and the stuff getting painted on top of it became as much the actual painting was. All five of the cameras were running time-lapse.

---

61 Kevin Hayden. Check out Phantogram's "When I'm Small" or Cardi B's "Bartier Cardi." Hayden served as Director of Photography for both and many, many more.

62 Ian Bavitz, b/k/a Aesop Rock.

ISAAC RAVISHANKARA, DIRECTOR, "ZERO DARK THIRTY:"

That left me with three days to finish the video. So, really quickly, I threw a cut together and got some notes. Locked down the edit of just him performing against white. Then, I kind of made a time-lapse of each camera angle. So you have to do five separate time-lapses. From there, I kind of messed around with scrubbing back and forth between time-lapses as if you're moving the dial on a QuickTime video scrubbing left and right, making it going forward and backward in time with the hit on the beat. I had kind of worked all of that out. Then, it was just a 48 hour haul in tracing every single frame. And there's ways you can kind of cheat it a little bit. But I didn't sleep for two straight days. It was just me in a room, tracing. And it's funny because if you watch it, the vibe feels good enough to carry you through it. The performance and everything like that. But when I see it, I see all the scenes. It's a really sloppy video. It's fine. It doesn't matter.

In almost any field, creators see blemishes in their work that no viewer notices. Ravishankara, who painstakingly shot, processed, and edited "Zero Dark Thirty" sees the rough edges, but can appreciate the viewer's love of the video.

ISAAC RAVISHANKARA, DIRECTOR, "ZERO DARK THIRTY:"

There's something nice about it where it feels kind of homemade. And you're seeing this guy paint this mural up and down. It feels really DIY. We've kind of leaned into that aesthetically.

As CORO's paintings and the song lyrics allude to the concept of extinction, the video also explores themes of fear and paranoia. Notice the shadowy figures passing by the newspapered-over windows.

ISAAC RAVISHANKARA, DIRECTOR, "ZERO DARK THIRTY:"

It wasn't something that came up initially, but then when we got to that space... I think it wasn't at that space, but as we were looking around warehouses in Oakland, I saw this thing of papered-over windows. When you're inside, it has a sort of great feeling of light coming in from the outside, but you don't know what's really happening. It became a really loose idea that he was hiding out in that space and hiding out in his thoughts. It feels exactly like the vibe of the song.

CORO, ARTIST, "ZERO DARK THIRTY:"

Anytime you see the windows, it looks like there's a bunch of people walking out front. Those were real people. That wasn't a theatrical prop. Those were people walking around. That was set on a major street that got a ton of foot traffic, so there were people walking by all of the time.

On occasion, I peruse the YouTube comments for videos. A solid 1% are legitimately funny. (Like 40% are a reference to the song being "real hip-hop" opposed to two or three artists the commenter dislikes.) Reading the comments for "Zero Dark Thirty" presented me with an unexpected idea.

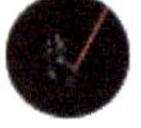

Gabriel C. 5 years ago

I'm I the only one who thinks he looks like Jimmy Fallon with a scruffy beard?

9 REPLY

tgms177 3 years ago

aesop rock looks like jimmy fallons older brother

503 REPLY

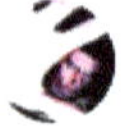

Random G 4 years ago

Jimmy Falon with a beard rapping?

63 REPLY

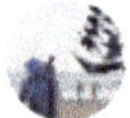

sublyme29 3 years ago

legit looks like jimmy fallon

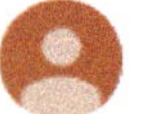

ais614bum 4 years ago

WHY DOES HE LOOK LIKE JIMMY FALLON AT 0:33?!!

2 REPLY

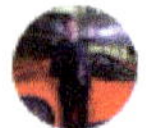

Nick Adkins 5 years ago

Jimmy Fallon with a beard.

Where I am not really seeing the resemblance, I asked Isaac.

Isaac Ravishankara, Director, "Zero Dark Thirty:" I mean kind of. It's funny. I had never seen him with a big beard like that in all the time I had seen him perform. I showed up. It was so last minute and thrown together that these videos happen on such a small budget. We slept at his house while we were there. He was like, "Hey, I've got a couch for you." It was definitely made that way. He's definitely one of the most self-conscious dudes I've ever met. I think that's where his mind's at, where his lyrics come from. He was growing out his beard while he was working on the album. He was like, "Should I shave it? Is it weird looking?" I was like, "No, man. It's awesome. It looks really cool." I think part of it also is that it's just him sitting on the floor. That makes him look smaller. That was intentional too. Having him hide out against this great mural. He's a big dude. Visually, he looks like Jimmy Fallon. If you saw them side-to-side, they feel like nothing alike. I bet he's 6-4, 6-5.[63]

63 A cursory Google search puts Fallon at 6'0". Not sure if this is barefoot or in Costanza Timberlands.

He's not super skinny either. It's funny, like I said I kind of came up with the 3OH!3 kids. Sean, the one I grew up with, is always called the short one but he's like a big 6-2. The tall one is like 6-8. Shooting videos with them is always really funny because 6'8" is just hard to shoot. We have to use stands and stuff to level them out.

ISAAC RAVISHANKARA, DIRECTOR, "ZERO DARK THIRTY:"

Those two videos are tied together.[64] Not just because they were artists I grew up listening to, and because I've always had an affinity for that side of hip-hop. It's also because they're on the same label., But also because this idea of trying to let the artist and the lyrics be enough and just looking at them I'm putting it in a more artistic context instead of just a basic rap video with rapping at camera. I was looking for a third way on both of these. Have something that artistically expresses the same sentiments the artist is trying to express but not try to over-reach it. Making something that supports the song. It was really nice to be able to do those two back-to-back. The Rhymesayers[65] people have always been the nicest people to work with. It's funny as there's this paradigm of rappers that in general are standoffish and hard. I've never worked with two nicer dudes than Ian and Sean[66].

ISAAC RAVISHANKARA, DIRECTOR, "ZERO DARK THIRTY:"

I think the funniest thing to me about the Aesop Rock video was just how crazy the whole thing came together. For me, it was a really amazing experience. There is sort of a teenage dream experience. I work with this guy I had listened to forever. Once I'd sort of moved on with the music I was listening to, getting that phone call and getting all giddy, hopping on the bus up to San Francisco, and meeting him for coffee and realizing that he has a home and I'm crashing on his couch. It was a really humbling thing.

CORO, ARTIST, "ZERO DARK THIRTY:"

It's funny. I hit Aesop up and said some dude hit me up about that video. I've actually had, over the

64 Aesop Rock's "Zero Dark Thirty" and Atmosphere's "The Last to Say."

65 Rhymesayers Entertainment, independent label based in Minneapolis. Started by Atmosphere members Slug and Ant, Musab, and Saddiq, Rhymesayers has been driven by Atmosphere but also released work from heavyweights Aesop Rock, MF DOOM, Evidence, Dilated Peoples, and Brother Ali.

66 Sean Daley, b/k/a Slug from Atmosphere.

years, more people hit me up about that video than any other music video I've ever done. It was a pretty well received video. I'm always kind of surprised. People are always like, "You did that 'Zero Dark Thirty' video," and I'm like "Wow! That's cool" Ian's got a pretty good following. He's a pretty well known dude. It trips me out as even years later, people remember that video. It's endured. We did a really similar thing with that "Get Out of the Car" video. It was almost the same thing. He had me draw a bunch of shit and Rob actually superimposed it on. Rob filmed him in a blank space rapping and he did a similar thing where I drew a bunch of stuff and time-lapsed it. This time I got to use my IPAD, so it was a little easier on my knees. I could just sit here and draw stuff and then send him the file. Rob put it all together in AfterEffects or whatever. It's kind of fun because it reminded me a lot of the ZD30 video in that it was sped-up shit happening around him.

ISAAC RAVISHANKARA, DIRECTOR, "ZERO DARK THIRTY:"

He was sarcastic and funny. The main thing that was hilarious, and I'll try to find some photos, we are in a room where the lighting has to be continuous. Totally constant when we were painting the mural. It's like 14 hours. We all wanted to be there. We didn't want to just leave the room. We had to check the cameras and stuff like that. We realized that very quickly it was just full of paint fumes. At the end of the first hour, we were all wearing gas masks. I'll find the photos. It's like five or six people against the wall wearing gas masks. Coro who always works with a gas mask on, on the other side just kind of painting away. Then every 10 or 15 minutes like,: "How about if we do this or this."

RAP'S BEST ZERO, DARK, (OR) THIRTY

Zero 7's Somersault Remix: By some randomness that I may need to detail in a separate oral history, Zero 7, Sia, MF DOOM, and Dangermouse combined to create this absolute gem, where DOOM's vocals detail the feelings of love in a surprisingly poignant way.[67]

0 to 100: That Frank Dukes beat. He did "Biking" too.

Zero Fux: Any Kool Keith fan can tell you that he's as good as he wants to be. Weirdly, he seems to be showing his greatest effort in years on an album[68] containing the chorus "We give Zero Fux."

---

67 Not because DOOM lacks talent in any way but because he generally does not seem to touch upon this topic.

68 KEITH, produced entirely by Beatnut Psycho Les.

La the Darkman: Want a good segue? "Zero Fux" features Cypress Hill's frontman B-Real. La's biggest look is arguably "Devil in a Blue Dress" on *Soul Assassins,* the excellent compilation produced by Cypress Hill's DJ Muggs.

Dark Time Sunshine: Emcee Onry Ozzborn and producer Zavala. It's not often where a listen to a computer generated playlist wholly commands my attention. When Spotify Recommends dropped "Instructions to Numb" on me, I almost had to pull over the car.

It's Dark and Hell Is Hot: Make sure you find the *Yesterday* parody where the world knows not of Dark Man X instead of the Beatles. What's the best song here- "Ruff Ryders Anthem," "Get At Me Dog," or "Stop Being Greedy?" I think with a gun to my head, I might have to go with SBG.

Dark Sky Paradise: Big Sean album features two super dope videos, the adorable Jhene Aiko assisted "I Know" and "Play No Games," an homage to the sitcom *Martin*, in which uber-talented psychopath Chris Brown appears to be acting in a different video. Even his madness can't ruin it. Great use of Drake and E-40 guest appearances.

30 Hours: Listen to Kanye's "30 Hours." Then check Arthur Russell's "Answers Me." Lastly, think about how dope it was that Kanye turned the latter into the former. Repeat a billion times until you happily pass away at age 130. Producer/drummer Karriem Riggins has a production credit on here. Did he play those drums? Because if so, bless you sir.

Deltron 3030: Del the Funkee Homosapien, producer Dan The Automater, and DJ Kid Koala. Their self-titled debut concept album is near-perfect. If you want to have a rapper talk about things where you have no idea what he's talking about it, Del is on the short list.[69] If you have to start with a song or two, I'd recommend "Positive Contact" and "Mastermind." Their follow-up was star-studded but not as magical. However, it does feature the Casual lyric "There's a pentagon in every pentagram. Do your geometry. It's in the center, fam."

CORO, ARTIST, "ZERO DARK THIRTY"

Oh my god, man. I was actually telling him earlier that I don't remember that much about that day because of that. When you write on the wall, you're breathing in. When I was a younger man, it was a little easier. But I got older and those fumes fuck with you dude. It really does. They got pretty blurry. I remember at the end, they had me spray paint some cat and some other shit that I don't even know if it made it in the video. It felt like a dream or something. I wore a mask too. Just indoors and that much paint.

---

69 MF DOOM and Pharoahe Monch are excellent too.

CORO, ARTIST, "ZERO DARK THIRTY:"

They all had shitty masks. You need the good masks. If I remember, they had to have someone go buy the good ones. They had those white "you're working out on the lawn" masks. You need a filter on it.

ISAAC RAVISHANKARA, DIRECTOR, "ZERO DARK THIRTY:"

We did it in cycles where we would shoot the whole thing, and then go outside for some fresh air. I've never really had an experience like that on set before. It looked as much like the end of the world that it was supposed to feel like.

CORO, ARTIST, "ZERO DARK THIRTY:"

I remember a couple of funny things happening, but I can't remember the details because of the fucking spraypaint honestly! So back behind this gallery, there was an outdoor restaurant. I remember going out there to take breaks and people being horrified. I remember people being really curious about what we were doing in there, because it smelled, and I'm progressively more and more covered in paint. We're smoking weed right out in the parking lot. We were the riff-raff. Like I said, I'm super vague on a lot of that. It was downtown Oakland. There was a First Fridays where all of the galleries open to get a lot of foot traffic. That was going on. There was a lot of foot traffic going on and that made it even weirder for me.

COUSINS

ATMOSPHERE: THE LAST TO SAY

AESOP ROCK: GET OUT OF THE CAR

PHANTOGRAM: WHEN I'M SMALL

GREAT GRAFFITI IN MUSIC VIDEOS

Aesop Rock: "No Jumper Cables" Director Joey Garfield inserts Aesop and collaborators Blockhead and Vast Aire into legendary hip-hop doc *Style Wars*. Weirdly seamless for a 2004 creation.

Company Flow: "End To End Burners" El-P, Mr. Len, and Big Jus represent all elements of hip-hop on the subway flanked by a three-dimensional burner.

Meyhem Lauren: "Got the Fever" A great deal of graffiti covers the "after," the product of writing. GTF is arguably rap's best look at the "during," what graffiti writing looks like in the moment of creation.

Promoe: "These Walls Don't Lie" Another 2004 video with dated yet ahead-of-its-time visual effects. This video features animated graffiti pieces on-wall to promote excellent Swedish emcee Promoe.

Artifacts: "Wrong Side of the Tracks" In 1994, another student in my dorm used to buy DJ Madsol[70] tapes. My memory may be off but I remember that on one tape, Madsol spun one loop of "Wrong Side of the Tracks," which we had not heard of at the time. Hearing such a small piece of one of rap's all-time beats, from slept-on T-Ray, was incredibly cruel. As the CD was not out at the time and if I remember correctly, the song was not labeled, we just had to wait and hope to cross paths with the song again. We did, of course, and the homage to writing features and aptly dope video.

---

70 DJ Madsol-Desar evolved into a dope producer, with credits like Laster's "Off Balance" and Talib Kweli's "Piece of Mind.".

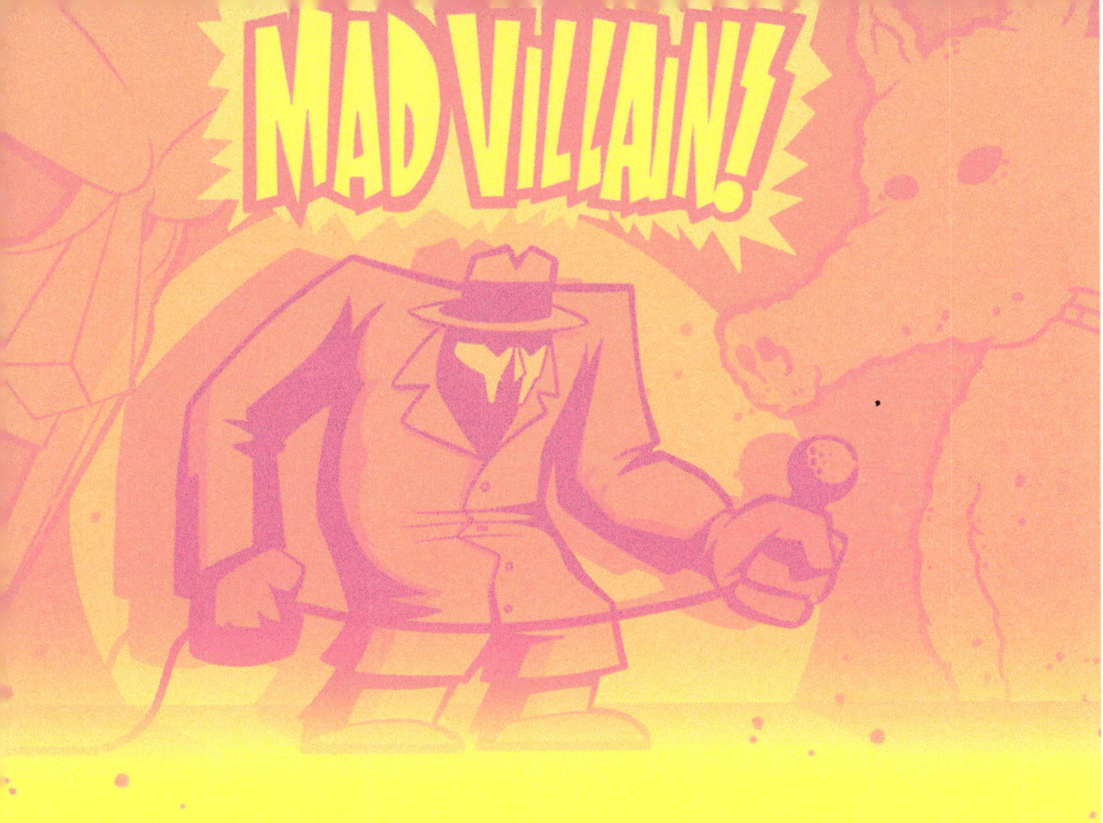

CHAPTER 7

MADVILLAIN: ALL CAPS

JAMES REITANO, DIRECTOR AND ANIMATOR, ON HIS HIP-HOP ORIGINS:

I met Chris[71] in the '90s. He's from the Bay Area so we knew each other through a few people, namely Kutmasta Kurt[72], who I grew up with. We grew up in Santa Cruz. We got involved in hip-hop when we were teenagers. I was the graffiti writer and he was a DJ. We've always remained friends throughout the years. The first video I ever did was actually for him. It was for him and Kool Keith, for their Masters of Illusion[73] record.

KUTMASTA KURT AND DAN THE AUTOMATER HATE EACH OTHER

James Reitano, Director and Animator: You could write a whole book on that whole situation with Keith and Automator and Kurt. There's quite a history there.

James Reitano, Director and Animator: We did a panel about 4 years ago for "Hip-Hop in Comics." I do it every year at Comic-Con and WonderCon. The guy who organizes it, Patrick74said "I want to get you on there but if you know anybody else, great, bring them on there too." I said, "I'll bring Kutmaster Kurt. He's in town and collects comics as well. So I bring him there and Automator's there by chance too. He's on the panel. These guys have not talked to each other in 12, 15 years. There's been lawsuits and all this shit. They literally sat on either ends of the table. It was pretty hilarious. I told him, "I had no idea he was going to be there." It worked out. They were fine. It was funny. I can feel the tension in the room. Chali 2na was like "that was kind of weird." That one had a really good audience. I think it was the first one that we did. It was a good turnout.

---

71 Chris Manak b/k/a Peanut Butter Wolf, artist and owner of Stones Throw, the label that released Madvillain's "Madvillainy." The label has helped launch and support the careers of countless artists including Madlib, Aloe Blacc, Homeboy Sandman, Mayer Hawthorne, J. Dilla, MF DOOM, Aesop Rock, and Oh No.

72 Kutmasta Kurt, DJ/producer with a unique, eclectic style, is best known for his collaborations with Kool Keith and Motion Man. Masters of Illusion is Kurt, Keith, and Motion.

73 The video is 2000's "We All Over."

74 Journalist Patrick A. Reed

JAMES REITANO, DIRECTOR AND ANIMATOR, ON CONNECTING TO STONES THROW:

I got into hip-hop in the early '80s. I got involved in graffiti art in the Bay Area. I was about 13 or 14. It became a big deal for all of us who got involved in Zulu Nation.[75] Then, in my mid-to-late teens, I kind of got a little bit out of it. I was a bit disillusioned and I got into punk rock. Got big-time into punk rock. But I always did graffiti. Graffiti was like my common denominator throughout all of that. Years later I got in touch with Kurt. I moved to LA and back then you would go to a Stones Throw party and there'd be like 20 people there. It would be literally the Beat Junkies[76], Jurassic 5, Dilated Peoples, Madlib, and Chris. That was it at the party. It was that kind of community. I remember thinking "this is kind of extraordinary." I got embroiled in that community of people. Stones Throw kind of split apart. There was a big kind of schism that happened about five years ago. It's still a very small community. I never imagined I would work with any of those guys so it's been great.

JAMES REITANO, DIRECTOR AND ANIMATOR, ON THE PROCESS:

Ultimately it's all put into digital. I never trained to be an animator. I just kind of got into it by accident. This was back in a time where every video was "start from scratch." Let's do a great concept. It was like, "Let's take Jack Kirby's art and make it animated. Let's do that. It would be so fun." Literally drawing every single frame with pen and ink. That's how that happened. You scan it in and you color it in the computer. My biggest concern is that I really wanted to make it look

---

75 Largely organized by Afrika Bambaataa, The Universal Zulu Nation promoted "knowledge, wisdom, understanding, freedom, justice, equality, peace, unity, love, respect, work, fun, overcoming the negative to the positive, economics, mathematics, science, life, truth, facts, faith, and the oneness of god." "Zulu Beliefs," *The Universal Zulu Nation*, 14 July 2020, Web.

76 I attended the University of Chicago from 1998 to 2002 and was lucky enough to co-host a fairly prominent college radio show on the excellent community-based WHPK. At that time, hosting one of the station's three hip-hop shows was a prestigious honor. For some context, we alternated Saturdays for a few months with Xtreme and Twilite Tone. Xtreme is an accomplished producer who produced Ghostface Killah's "Back Like That" Twilite Tone raps under the alias Ynot and traded lines with Common on the absolute Classic "Chapter 13." I hold an enormous amount of gratitude for my close college friend Vinod Ponusammy, V Funk for radio purposes, who acquired our air time and brought me on to cohost. I don't think anything could have been more fun to me at that time than hosting this show. We were visited by MF DOOM, Copywrite, Camu Tao, Jakii, Oldominion, and even Skee-Lo. My favorite moment though was when our show was taken over by the World Famous Beat Junkies. J-Rocc hosted in the booth with us as various member DJs occupied the four turntable setup. I have a memory of a routine where the two DJs juggled Jeru's "Can't Stop the Prophet Remix" and then spun in the original. Legendary. For every positive thing Vinod has brought into my life, he lost the DAT recording we made of that day. That was unforgivable.

tangible. I didn't want it to look like Flash[77], which people were using at the time to animate. I really wanted to make it look like paper was moving. I had two months to do it. It took three months. Back then, Stones Throw didn't have any video budget. They didn't have anything. Chris paid me out of his personal account. "Can you make this work?" "I'll make it work."

JAMES REITANO, DIRECTOR AND ANIMATOR, ON CONNECTING TO DOOM THROUGH COMICS:

It was a lot of fun once that started to become the concept. Cool, fun stuff with actual paper. I'm a huge Silver-Age[78] Marvel Comics guy. I have a huge collection of them that I'm actually looking at right now. I talked to DOOM[79] when we were starting to do it. I had a phone conversation with him. He was like "Remember that issue of Fantastic Four where Quasimoto fought the Mad Thinker? When you meet someone and you start talking about that kind of stuff, it's almost like you were in the same frat or something. We just hit it off. That enthusiasm fueled the project. More times than not, you deal with someone who's like ,"Hey, I might do a video with you that's about action figures," and they say, "I don't give a fuck about action figures." It's not the same. When someone's really into it, you really want to try. That's how this was. That's why it came off how it did, even though I was never happy with it.

JAMES REITANO, DIRECTOR AND ANIMATOR, ON THE PROPOSED "ALL CAPS" REBOOT:

On the 10-year anniversary of "All Caps," I pitched Stones Throw with reenacting the video but with little kids dressing up. Doing a dramatization with a chubby kid in the Doom suit. The whole thing but with cardboard. It never happened, but I thought that would be so fun.

JAMES REITANO, DIRECTOR AND ANIMATOR, ON MEETING THE ELUSIVE DOOM IN THE WILD:

I met [DOOM] at the Stones Throw house. They used to all live together- Madlib, Jeff[80], and Chris, and Egon[81]. We'd just go over there and hang out. I had about two years where I was always doing

---

77 Adobe Flash.

78 According to web conglomerate Google, the Silver Age ran from 1956-1970,.

79 Emcee MF DOOM and producer Madlib are Madvillain.

80 Stones Throw's art & web director, Jeff Jank. Feel free to google "Jeff Jank album cover." His best cover might be the classically simple, mysterious *Madvillainy*.

81 Egon served as GM at Stones Throw from 2000 to 2011. During that time, he created a reissue based label called Now-Again Records, which became independent in 2012. He is integral to the work of production legends Dilla and Madlib, serving as creative director of the J. Dilla Estate and a partner in Madlib Invazion.

projects for them. This was just before that. I was hanging out with Chris all the time. We ended up becoming really good friends after a while. It was really cool. Right around that time, I went over to talk to him about the project, like I just want to make sure we all understand what we're doing here. DOOM happened to be there. I didn't know it was him. I just see this guy behind me. He's like, "Hey how's it going?" I'm like, "Oh, great." Later on, someone told me "Yeah, that's him." I was like "Really?!" It was essentially a quick handshake, and then he was off doing things with Madlib. They were working on that actual record at the time. Then we had the phone conversation where I was really talking to him about it specifically.

Silver-age Marvel Comics contained memorable advertisements. So memorable that "All Caps" contains several homages to them.

JAMES REITANO, DIRECTOR AND ANIMATOR:

That was an homage to all the ads in the '70s. We had to put that in there because it was in every Marvel Comic in the '70's.

At 0:44, the video features an ad for "New Super Sea-Chimps."

JAMES REITANO, DIRECTOR AND ANIMATOR:

These brine shrimp that you'd order. Those ads made it seem like they were going to be these cartoon characters but when they arrived., they were kind of a joke.

At 0:47, the video features an ad for a "High Paying Job in Electronics." DOOM's lyrics are scrawled on the address form, "As he utters the calm flow. Don't talk about my moms Yo!" The ad features a bookish type character.

JAMES REITANO, DIRECTOR AND ANIMATOR:

That's my friend Dean.[82] Dean and I did the Motion Man music video together. He's an interesting character. I worked with him at a place called Den, which was a dot com entertainment network. I made a hip-hop show there. I met Chris through that hip-hop show. Dean had the punk rock show so we became really good friends. He's an old veteran of LA punk bands like The Motels and Code Blue. That was his background so we just became friends from working together. I said to him "You have to be in this ad." He was like, "Great I have all the clothes." That's how that came about.

82 Dean Chamberlain, also a member of the Ju Ju Hounds.

At 1:35, an advertisement for J-Tel Records, promising 12 Smash Hits for $3.99, features a man sitting with a guitar.

JAMES REITANO, DIRECTOR AND ANIMATOR:

All the K-Tel Records in the 70's. That's me sitting there with a wig on.[83]

At 1:37, "Sell Seeds, Get Prizes."

JAMES REITANO, DIRECTOR AND ANIMATOR:

Every Marvel Comic in the 70's had the 'Get Prizes' ad. Then, the kids that are in that are Dean's nephews. The African-American kid, I can't remember his name. He was a friend's son who was in the Motion Man video[84] as well. We had done the Motion Man video about six months before with the action figures. A lot of those same people carried into this.

While the "All Caps" video is brilliantly conceived and executed, the streaming versions found online are less than the highest resolution. It's unclear whether the "Mail to the Villain" page features real letters or Lorem ipsum-esque gibberish.

JAMES REITANO, DIRECTOR AND ANIMATOR:

They are not gibberish. Jeff from the label gave me stuff for that because we talked about that. I said, "Hey. I'm going to do a letters page. Should I just put stuff in there?" He said, "Yeah, put this in there." I think it might have been a fan letter Stones Throw got. They do, in fact, say, "Dear Stones Throw, Man. I bought two copies of the third issue of Madvillain. I'm happy to say that it's a good book, but how come blah blah blah that DOOM." This is all just me writing bullshit. The first letter says "I bought two." I repeated a lot of shit there. Crystal Schurmer, that's my ex-girlfriend. I put a letter that she wrote in there. She helped me animate this. These letters are actually real, but I can barely see anything. I just made up a bunch of goofy shit.

Keen viewers of "All Caps" will notice that the video ends on a cliffhanger.

JAMES REITANO, DIRECTOR AND ANIMATOR:

We kept it open like that. I thought it would be fun. Everybody talked about doing that. "Oh god!

---

83 When confronted with the fact that he looked like Tom Petty, Reitano laughed.

84 Motion Man's "Clearing The Field."

You gotta do a series of these." I think that was the plan. We did in a way. I think I did a MySpace page artwork for them after that. We did the action figures of course. We continued on the action figure box. But never in any sort of media.

"All Caps" was popular enough that Kidrobot, best known for creating stylish vinyl toys, created a Madvillain figure. At the time of writing, the last completed Ebay listing for the toy, in new condition, was $249+$25 shipping.

JAMES REITANO, DIRECTOR AND ANIMATOR:

They were fun. The first one was something they were just doing as a joke like, "Let's make him an action figure." I think Kidrobot had pitched in to Stones Throw, so they did it and they sold like, "Oh shit! People buy these types of things?" That was the first one. The second one I did with Egon at rappcats, outside of Stones Throw. That became kind of a problem as Chris was like, "Hey, how come you didn't talk to us?" That ended up being kind of a bummer, but we did the two.

JAMES REITANO, DIRECTOR AND ANIMATOR, ON THE DOORS OPENED BY "ALL CAPS":

It's 2003 so that was a lifetime ago. Everyone wanted to work with me right after that. That was one of those weird Hollywood experiences where the phone didn't stop ringing. It was my first experience with that. I got brought on to The Director's Bureau, Roman Coppola's music video shop. I stuck with them for a while. It was an odd time because all of a sudden… It's not funny, but this was kind of a crazy thing. These guys from the agency, Goodby & Silverstein, an ad agency. They had called me and said "Hey, we want to work with you. We want to do something like an animated comic book. So, we are working with Hewlett Packard, and we have Serena Williams. They are going to do an ad together and they like the 'All Caps' video. We want to do something similar." So they said, "But it's gotta be for a billboard, an animated billboard." So I thought, "Oh Jesus, man." "Oh we need it in three weeks." It's the biggest thing I've ever done in terms of score. It was a little bit of a nightmare because I've never done something that big in such a short amount of time. But it worked out and I got paid a shit ton of money. That was one of the bigger things that came out of it. Working with Cartoon Network and Aqua Teen Hunger Force[85] came out of "All Caps." It's run the gamut.

85 For my money, ATHF is easily the funniest absurdist cartoon. Plus, the characters' appearances on "Danger Doom" were executed perfectly. Carl has one of TV's best surnames, Brutananadilewski.

THE GENIUS OF PEANUT BUTTER WOLF

Peanut Butter Wolf has established a reputation of unearthing musical gold from unexpected places. He released early work from Mayer Hawthorne, whose original intention for singing was to create material to sample. Stones Throw released the singing debut of an unheralded rapper named Aloe Blacc. He also put his neck out to release Madlib's alter-ego Quasimoto.

James Reitano, Director and Animator: Yeah, that's true. He had done it and not taken it very seriously. Chris had heard it and that was Chris's genius. He was a true believer, like, "We've got to put this out!" Otis was like, "Okay, whatever you want to do." That's how that label became what it was. It was Chris being that way about everything. He had a lot of misses but when he heard something and liked it, he was 100%. I have such admiration for that guy. He came to our wedding. He was really one of those people who I looked at as a mentor even though we're the same age. He just put his money where his mouth was and said "Okay, we said we're gonna do this. Let's do this." We were gonna do an animated feature film. We met for about two months, almost twice a week, me, him, and Madlib. We were gonna do an animated feature, kind of like a French style animation. I had these whole scripts. I was writing with a friend of mine. We were totally into it. It never panned out, and the Quasimoto video came out of that. I took a lot of the elements from that into the Czarface, put some into a video I did for Skrillex a few years ago. I've cannibalized a lot of it and Chris even said, "You put some of that stuff in the video!" I said, "That was ten years ago. There's a statute of limitations there." Donuts was going to be the same thing for Dilla, a throwaway thing. No one listens to beat tapes. I was like "I do!"

JAMES REITANO, DIRECTOR AND ANIMATOR, ON BUILDING HIS CATALOGUE:

I directed the Danger Doom song, not the seminal Adult Swim show. They had no time. They had a ton of money but no time. I thought, "I can do this." I just got done doing a movie for Fox Sports. That's a crazy fucking year. I did the "Stat" Cut Chemist video and we just decided to end it in the middle because neither of us were happy. Then the Quasimoto video[86] happened. I've got this movie to make. I've still got a full time job at this place called iFilm. Then, did the Aqua Teen Hunger Force video in October. It was a crazy fucking year. My dad got sick. It was this whole nutty year. Lo and behold, the next year I see Cut Chemist at an art gallery, and he said "We really need to finish that video, so let's do it. Same price." We finished it. That was awesome. It was so fun to do a turntable video because I've always loved turntablism. But to do something that was instrumental was challenging. But I thought, "This is going to be great, because I've never saw this."

---

86 "Bullyshit"

JAMES REITANO, DIRECTOR AND ANIMATOR, ON WORKING WITH CUT CHEMIST:

He's an interesting character. We recently worked together on this Biz Markie video. He's funny because he was micromanaging the character design process. To do that, you make it difficult for the director to animate. When I do a character design, it's kind of like, "You can change the clothes and the color and everything else, but this is what we have to work with." Because if you want to give me your nephew's crayon drawing, I'm not going to be able to move that. He was really micromanaging the designs of the turntables, and that's part of the reason we ended it. I said, "We gotta compromise on this." He said, "I want this to be just like my drawing with colored pencils. It needs to look like that." He was really adamant about it. Then he says, "Hey, look man. I was an animation major at UCLA. I get too into this shit, so just tell me to shut the fuck up." I was like "We're not doing it because of this." And he understood. He was an animation major, and I've never dealt with an animator. Usually, they're like, "Do your thing!" I worked with Czarface just now. That was great. They said "Here. Do what you gotta do, and we will see you in March!" We just delivered that.

JAMES REITANO, DIRECTOR AND ANIMATOR, ON THE POPULARITY OF "ALL CAPS":

You get tired about everyone talking about it. The fact that you were in Happy Days and everything after Happy Days, no one gives a fuck about. They just want to talk to you about what it was like to work with Fonzie. There's that. That's something that I ran into but I've gotten to work with so many awesome people since. I like DOOM but I really love Madlib's music. Someone gave me the Quasimoto instrumental, and I'm thinking, "This is fucking amazing." I'm thinking, "This guy gets it. This is what I've been waiting for." I like RZA's production, but this guy's stuff is something else. It's why I messaged Chris out of the blue like "I met you a few years ago. How about I do something with Madlib, and we make it look like an old cheap Marvel cartoon from the '60's when they would just move the comic book pages?" He said, "Let's do that! Sounds great. Let's do it for the song Money Folder that DOOM and Madlib happen to be working on right now." It was going to be that and then it changed.

JAMES REITANO, DIRECTOR AND ANIMATOR, ON THE PERKS OF WORKING WITH STONES THROW:

When I first met Madlib and I was going to work on this project, they gave me like eight CDs of just his beats. Those became like albums for me. I still have them and still listen to them from time to time. There's 600 beats and a lot of those became the Jaylib record, the Madvillain record. Those minute and a half, two minute beats. So when they came out with Donuts, it was great.

COUSINS

DANGERDOOM: ATHF

QUASIMOTO: BULLYSHIT

MOTION MAN: C'MON Y'ALL

GREAT ANIMATED VIDEOS

Your Old Droog: We Don't Know You (Dir: Sean Tyler Ferguson)

KOOL AD: Hickory (Dir: Youth Experimental Studio)

Das Racist: Who's That? Brooown! (Dir: Thomas DeNapoli)

Samiyam f/ Earl Sweatshirt: Mirror (Dir: Ruff Mercy)

Super BWE + Chance the Rapper: Fool Wit It Remix (Dir: Abel Gray)
Deca: Waiting (Dir: Deca)

Madvillain: All Caps (Dir: James Reitano)

J. Rawls f/ J-Live: Great Live Caper (Dir: ?)

Lil' Dicky f/ Snoop Dogg: Professional Rapper (Dir: Douglas Einar Olsen)

Madlib: Slim's Return (Dir: David Ahuja)

SELECT JAMES REITANO VIDEOS

Quasimoto: Bullyshit

14K: Five & Ten

Mayer Hawthorne: Robot Love

Madlib: Beat Konducta In India

Biz Markie: La Da Da

Danger Doom: Aqua Teen Hunger Force

Masters of Illusion: We All Over

Mayer Hawthorne: I Wish It Would Rain (Dir: Henry DeMaio, Animated by James Reitano)

DJ Nu-Mark: Tonight (Dir: Odin Wadleigh, Animated by James Reitano)

Cut Chemist: Spat

Czarface: Mettle With Metal

Motion Man: C'Mon Y'all

James Reitano, Director and Animator: That was [Kutmasta] Kurt saying, "Can we do something with this [song]?" We did the packaging, the video, and everything else. That was the first live action thing I had done, and it was really fucking difficult. It was a lot of work. It took nine months to do that, and I just learned a lot. We hired a Director of Photography for that, believe it or not. Had to get all of these things made, and had all of these kids do it for us. We had to get locations. I was like, "there is a real artform to this." That was a real learning experience for me.

James Reitano, Director and Animator, on the video's filming techniques: A lot of stop motion, and because we had a lot of digital tools, we did a lot of puppetry. We removed the things that we had attached to the figures. We had these rods we moved them with and we just digitally removed the rods. That's what we did with that one. A little bit of stop motion but not too much.

James Reitano, Director and Animator, on Motion Man: I've known him forever. He was in a group called Zero Tolerance back in the 90's. He's a real character. There's probably a bunch. This isn't my story but it's the story from the record. Motion Man is talking about being on tour with Kurt and Kurt's really hairy. Whenever they would share a shower, Motion Man would complain because he'd be covered in Kurt's fur. Paul's a great guy. I'm in touch with him still.

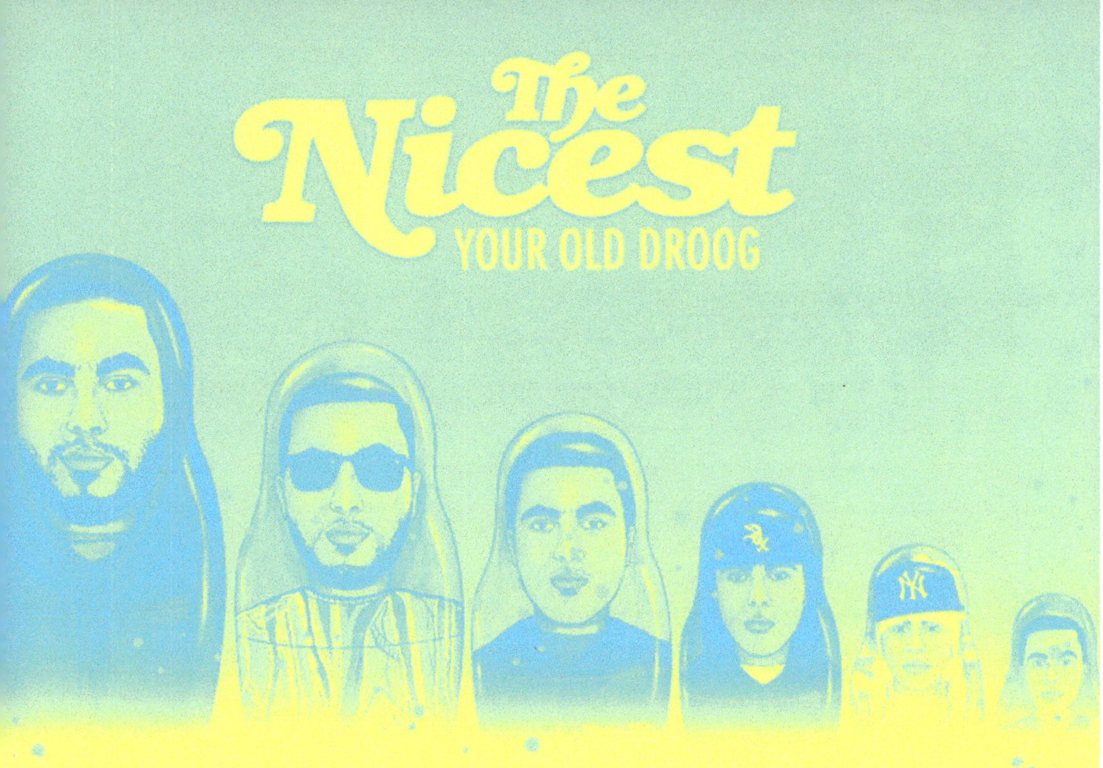

CHAPTER 8

YOUR OLD DROOG:
WE DON'T KNOW YOU

SEAN TYLER FERGUSON, DIRECTOR, ON CONNECTING TO DROOG:

The production company I worked for, Scheme Engine, was the in-house team for Roc Nation[87], Jay-Z's company. Within that network we were allowed access to athletes[88], musicians[89], philanthropists, artists, chefs; they've got the whole spectrum of media covered. There just happened to be a day where a friend of Droog's manager was in the office, and they had a bit of money and they wanted something, so we connected. It happened from there.

SEAN TYLER FERGUSON, DIRECTOR, ON HIS CREATIVE PROCESS:

It was a feeling. I was given two songs and I picked "We Don't Know You." I sat down outside of Tompkins Square Park[90] one day at a cafe and listened to the songs on repeat. I came up with a shot list and storyboard, shot-for-shot while enjoying some coffee and marijuana. I worked back and forth with Droog directly. He was very constructive. One thing that was fun was that he kept on wanting to make it raunchier. Did you notice there's rats fucking in one scene, and a blunt and 40 oz on the table in another? He wanted as much of that shit as possible which just added to the playfulness. He definitely gave it that tone of being edgy and grungy.

---

87 Entertainment company founded by Jay-Z in 2008. Roc Nation does almost everything. The Roc Nation site lists "artist management, music publishing, touring, production, strategic brand development and beyond."

88 Andre Ward, Robinson Cano, Yoenis Cespedes, Kyrie Irving, Caris Levert, Justise Winslow, Rudy Gay, Skyler Diggins, Dez Bryant, Juju Smith-Schuster, Leonard Fournette, Ndamukong Suh, Todd Gurley, Saquon Barkley, Victor Cruz among many more.

89 Alicia Keys, Benny the Butcher, Big Sean, Damian Marley, DJ Khaled, Fat Joe, J. Cole, Jadakiss, Jay Electronica, Jay-Z, Jim Jones, Kelly Rowland, Lil Uzi Vert, Ludwig Goransson, Mack Wilds, Mariah Carey, Miguel, Rapsody, Rihanna, Robin Thicke, Shakira, Statik Selektah, The Lox, Vic Mensah, Westside Gunn and MANY MORE!

90 NYC park located in the East Village, bordered by Avenue A, East 7th Street, Avenue B, and East 10th Street. While currently considered to be a generally safe park, Tompkins Square has had a history of unrest, including riots and high drug use. If you want to totally ruin your day, google "The Butcher of Tompkins Square."

SEAN TYLER FERGUSON, DIRECTOR, ON INTENTIONALITY:

Everything was thought out: color palette[91], setting, narrative, frame-rate, style. The message of the song is: now that Droog has made it, all these former acquaintances want special access and treatment, but it's not a real relationship. I wanted to convey the way Droog felt writing the song in as many ways as possible throughout the video.

With its beautiful color scheme, steady movement, and sense of infinity, "We Don't Know You" is among the easiest videos to watch. Oftentimes, such visual beauty is the entire premise of the video. When viewing "We Don't Know You," the viewer, caught up in the video's beauty, may miss the video's brilliant premise.

SEAN TYLER FERGUSON, DIRECTOR, ON THE VIDEO'S SYMBOLISM:

There was a lot of intent. He is always moving forward and rising up. He is from Coney Island, and we wanted to start with him and his roots. We opened with an emblematic NYC shot and made it look like he was in Brooklyn with the city in the distance. We wanted to visually represent his rise in the world starting from Coney Island, to Manhattan on his way to a recording studio in the second verse. In the third verse he's only represented in other forms of media, whether it's posters or television, to show the separation he now has from fans. I wanted to do little things like that to give it a narrative arc.[92]

SEAN TYLER FERGUSON, DIRECTOR, ON CREATING DETAIL:

I've always been inspired by title sequences in great films. After you watch a TV show or movie, when you go back and watch the title sequence with fresh eyes, there's so much in there you begin to appreciate. It tells you what's going to happen before you even see the outcome. You can usually pick it up, start to finish. I try to put that kind of mentality into my work, where you are adding in more detail than necessary in order to effectively communicate.

---

91 Author's note: Rap videos don't do enough with color. WDKY might be the best colored video in history.

92 Spelled out for the tired reader: In the first verse, Droog, a native of Brooklyn, is accessible in his NYC neighborhood. In the second verse, he is shown moving, to signify his career's movement. In the third verse, Droog, having made it is only accessible to the viewer through the media and not in person.

SEAN TYLER FERGUSON, DIRECTOR, ON HIS BARGAIN RATE:

Because it was a personal connection, we did the video for 5K, and for a two-month production, that's unheard of. It's really a luxury to be able to have the opportunity to put your time and focus on something whole-heartedly.

STF ON HIS INFLUENCES.

Sean Tyler Ferguson, Director: Definitely, my dad is the one who drove the love of film into me. My parents are both high school teachers for many years, and taught in Japan for 27 years, which is where I was born and raised. We watched old films together. We covered all of cinema history. He has an Excel spreadsheet that has thousands of movies, all ranked by genre, stars, descriptions, everything. He watches movies twice, one time for the narrative, and the second time the timing, wide shot, close up. Even though he's not a director, he's a biology teacher, he has that kind of approach. I've been raised on a counter to mainstream Hollywood. While I can still appreciate that, that is where my love of film and cinema came from.

You were an animator and raised in Japan, you must love anime. I never took to it. I'm not interested in it. I've never really seen any of it.

SEAN TYLER FERGUSON, DIRECTOR, ON MOTION GRAPHICS ANIMATION:

We did a one-day green-screen shoot. It was myself and two co-workers with a shopping cart dolly that we were pushing back and forth to get his walking shots. It was really simple. Everything else is composited. So it's not traditional animation, not frame-by-frame.

I'm actually going in and making these scenes kind-of like a shoebox-diorama. It allows for a lot of flexibility down the line where I can access each piece and add it or remove it at will. When it came to addressing the video at a third-draft stage, we could really go in and dissect it. It kind of speaks to the reason I got into motion graphics animation in the first place. I love film, but I just hate actors, and I don't enjoy dealing with live sets. It's a pain in the ass not being able to edit reality.

SEAN TYLER FERGUSON, DIRECTOR, ON YOUR OLD DROOG:

He's the working man's Nas. He got famous because everyone thought he was Nas under some mystery name.[93]

Sean Tyler Ferguson brilliantly illustrates the song's title during the chorus after the second verse. Whereas the first chorus had Droog physically welcoming the viewer into his world, the next chorus features Droog as the bouncer in front of the club. The movement is backward as he is bouncing the viewer through an infinite set of doors.

SEAN TYLER FERGUSON, DIRECTOR, ON CONSISTENCY OF MESSAGE:

Yeah, 'We don't know you.' Then, the last door closes and it hard-cuts to him in a poster. That's the distance you now have. You only see him in the media.

SEAN TYLER FERGUSON, DIRECTOR, ON DROOG'S PERSONALITY:

It's fun working with Droog. He's a goofy guy. You wouldn't think it. He walks into the room and has a very big presence. But he's fun and doesn't take himself too seriously.

SEAN TYLER FERGUSON, DIRECTOR, ON AN EASTER EGG:

One thing I was probably most proud of that most people don't catch is in the opening shot where you have the street signs. It says GOTTOH AVE. and THENICE ST. That reads "Got To Have The Nicest," which is the name of his album. I was trying hard to get that in there.

COUSINS

HIP-HOP QUIPS (2012)

AUDIEN: SOMETHING BETTER (LYRIC VIDEO)

MELO-X: FFFS

---

93 See insert below: The Original Mystery of YOD.

THE ORIGINAL MYSTERY OF YOD

In 2014, Your Old Droog uploaded his self-titled EP to Soundcloud. Diehard hip-hop fans couldn't help noticing that Your Old Droog sounded like Nas. Considering that such high quality work came from a then unknown with no known photograph, this premise was not ludicrous. People speculated on the potential motives. Maybe Nas could exert greater creative control outside of label constraints? Maybe Nas was hoping to generate buzz through a unique release? Eventually, we would learn that YOD was not Nas, and instead a Ukranian-born Brooklynite. But not before Nas had a brilliant moment with MTV's Rob Markman.[94]

RM: "There's a guy called Your Old Droog, who put a record out. And there's these conspiracy theories that they think it's a secret Nas album. People have pitched up the record and pitched down the record.

Nas: What do you mean a secret Nas album?

RM: There's an artist from Brooklyn. And his name is Your Old Droog and he put a record out. An album. And there's these conspiracy theories online. People think he's you. People think he sounds like you.

Nas: I have no idea what you're talking about.

RM: Nah, you never heard of it?

Nas: No.

RM: It's crazy on Twitter. It's like a sub-internet thing that's like blowing up. It's amazing. He did a show. He's clearly not you. You don't know about it. It's not you but for the record, you didn't put out a secret EP at all this year?

Nas: Who me? (laughing) I don't even know what that means. Nah. No. No secret EPs. I don't want a secret EP. I want you to know it's me when I drop.

The level of confusion from Nas in this segment is amazing to watch!

---

94 http://www.mtv.com/news/1947013/nas-responds-your-old-droog-rumors/

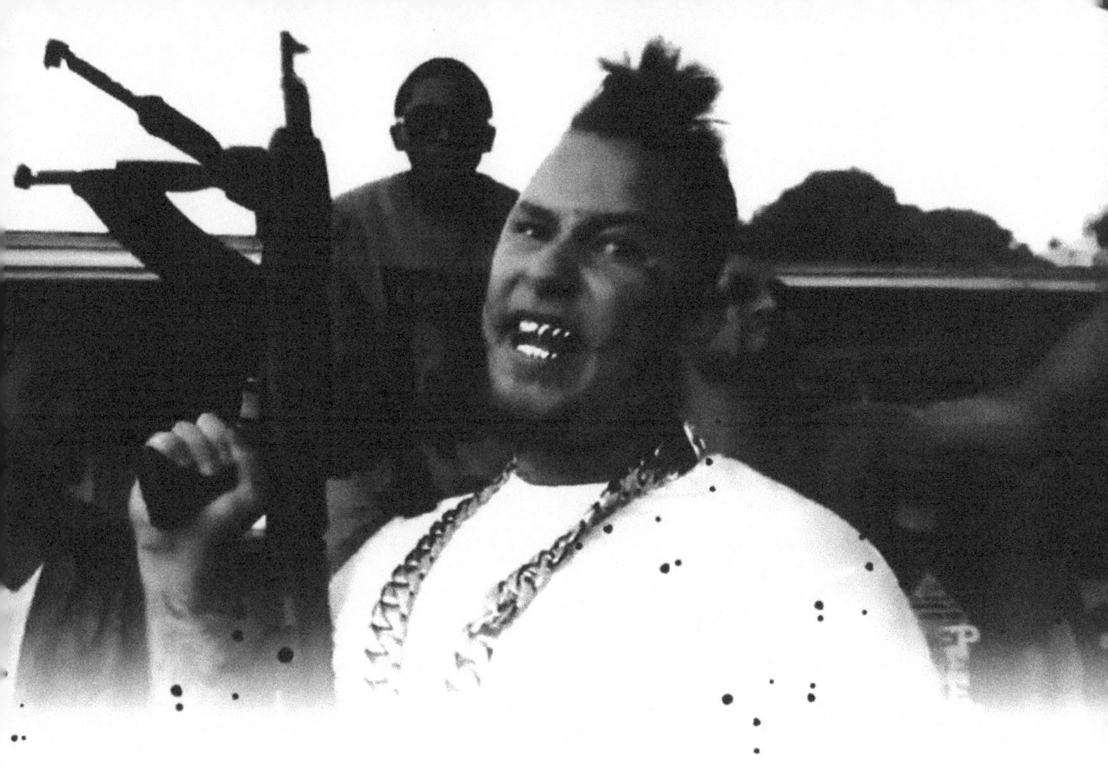

CHAPTER 9

STITCHES: BRICK IN YO FACE

MAZADI VISION, DIRECTOR:

Let me give you the actual version of how this all unfolded. Stitches, a/k/a Philip[95], his brothers were good friends of mine growing up. I had done some videos for Stitches in his younger years. I've been in the film game for about 12 years. His brothers were good friends of mine.

MAZADI VISION, DIRECTOR:

For quite some time, his brothers used to own a vapor shop. I'm there just hanging out. Phil was like "Can we do a video?" I'm like "What are we talking about?" He showed me the song. At first, I was like "What the fuck? Are you crazy? Are you joking? I remember Phil telling me, "I want to push this." I was kind of skeptical about the whole situation. I still really wasn't completely sold on it. He was like, "I'll shoot[96] you X amount of dollars, some quick cash, and we'll shoot in the next two days." I was like "Alright, cool. We'll shoot." I went home and I thought about it. I was like, "If we got to do this like this, we got to go balls to the wall and be ridiculously uncensored." We brainstormed the next day and went through some ideas. My partner and I found a camera and went around Miami and figured we'll find what we'll find. "Let's photo this abandoned house. We could do this. Let's get this mask. Let's create a story or a personality behind this mask." We shot it all in one day. We got in the car. We had no direct plan. We usually have a storyboard. We didn't have the direction where we would go. This wasn't a completed plan. We went to see some of his friends who were in the hood. All of the weaponry that you do see is a hundred percent real. We got it a little bit closer to who he exposes himself to be on a daily basis, who he chills with, who he's around with. Again the masked man. That was something that happened organically. It was more like, "Oh, shit! There's a mask there. Let's grab it. We can use it.

MAZADI VISION, DIRECTOR:

From a creative side, production side, I was like I don't know what we're going to do with this. Let's make something out of nothing. I gave it to my partner. He basically put his touches on it. He gave the final finish on it. I shot it. The intensity of it. In your face. All the visuals that you see was on me, but the actual creative post-production part of it, to bring it all together, my partner

95 Phillip Katsabanis

96 I love the fact that Stitches finds unique ways to use the verb "shoot."

did a phenomenal job. Especially when it says the little detail where the text says "BLOW," the font is actually the same font from the movie Blow. Those little details are kind of the things that we wanted to put out there. Especially as this is one of the lower budget videos I ever made in my life.

MAZADI VISION, DIRECTOR:

How it all unfolded, how it went viral from one day to the next, was pretty impressive. It was cool, but it was all organic. Nothing was planned. We just went out there. I had an idea. I wasn't about it at first. I went home and thought about it like "Fuck it. Do I have to be crazy to do this?"

MAZADI VISION, DIRECTOR:

You talking about the slow motion parts? When he throws the powder and hits the wall? We did change the frame rates. It's a combination of both post and camera work. I'm a Steadicam operator so we shot it on a Steadicam. As well as what is called ramping in the footage, in the post-production world. We go slow and then go fast. It gives it that jittery feel in an intense environment. Especially for the Hellraiser part, we felt like it was very important to play with the glitch of the actual mask and intensify his overall look and overall persona.

MAZADI VISION, DIRECTOR:

I don't have the exact numbers but it was within 2 weeks tops [that it hit 1,000,000 views.] We uploaded it on Worldstar. Once we got on Worldstar, the number started climbing. The YouTube numbers don't even reflect the actual numbers. The first platform was Worldstar which pushed it. Unless you clicked on the actual YouTube itself, it's not gonna reflect on the actual viewership. A lot of people must have gone back and seen it again. Our first marketing push was toward Worldstar alone. I think the Worldstar alone was at like 3 million, something ridiculous like that within the first week. It went viral from that point on. Obviously everyone was talking about Stitches being on Worldstar. It was a great decision by Stitches himself. A lot of people put things on Worldstar too and it doesn't hit like that. Waking up every day and seeing the numbers jump up another 100,000 was like "Wow. People are really loving the video."

MAZADI VISION, DIRECTOR:

Yes, it was a lesson. I learned a lot from that experience overall. What I mean by that is "It's what the people want." Again, I don't put my name on this video. It's not where my direction overall from my career has gone and where it's at right now. It has so many views on this one video. It's not that I'm not proud of it, It's just I'm not in the center of it. It basically made me pay a little bit more detail about what people want, what people are listening to. Dumb it down a little bit, and it makes it simpler, easier for everybody when you're not so complex in the editing. Keep that shock factor. We didn't create anything revolutionary. We just kept that shock factor that everybody was more than ready for.

MAZADI VISION, DIRECTOR:

First and foremost, I have a very vast group of friends. I'm not saying I'm from the hood. So going through those experiences and going to these houses, when you see the guy with the mask throwing the powder on the wall, that's a house that we found. We just walked up in there. We went in guerilla style and shot it. It's a broke down, abandoned house in the middle of the hood. We have all this camera equipment and people are trying to find out what we're doing in there. All of a sudden, Stitches comes out. This is obviously before he got all his notoriety and everybody who came up to us was mean-muggin' us and wanted to cause problems. And then, they're like, "Oh, you're going to be on Worldstar! Oh, hell yeah!" And they all jumped into the video. Because of that interaction, it made it cool. We were able to create more of a gang environment. That was one of the funniest things that happened. Obviously, Stitches is a clown so people that would walk by would scream at him, this and that. Those little moments. I think, overall, the one that had the biggest influence is when you're like "Oh, shit, I'm in the wrong place at the wrong time," but that it ends up working out for you. When people are acting like the thugs of the world and then you tell him you are doing some video for Worldstar, they're now like your best friends. That was a cool moment when we were in the wrong place at the wrong time, but we said the right things at the right time.

MAZADI VISION, DIRECTOR:

That was not Stitches in the mask. That was actually a good friend of Stitches who is actually doing time for murder right now at the moment. Two weeks after the video was released, he got sentenced. I believe he said that in the documentary for Vice. He was in trouble at the time, and he's like "I want to do this," and he just put the mask on and that was it. The idea was for him to be in the back while Stitches was rapping but we thought that would be corny. So we decided to have his own shot. A lot of people probably think that was Stitches, but it wasn't Stitches. It was his best friend who's doing time at the moment.

MAZADI VISION, DIRECTOR:

The guys I respect in the game that influenced me did not influence me on this video in any way. Because this was completely out of the element of what I like to put out there. I felt from a visual standpoint, let's intensify all of these shots and make sure they are in your face at all times. There was no influence on... I wasn't trying to edit it in any way inspired by any editing from any other video. All I was trying to do was make sure Stitches looked as grimy and as crazy as possible. For every edit cut that I did, there was not a millisecond where he looked away from the camera and looked weak or wasn't in character to look crazy. I made sure every second that I cut, with every shot, he embodied the energy of the craziness.

MAZADI VISION, DIRECTOR:

I appreciate you noticing that. You can tell the intensity we were trying to achieve. We definitely hit it on the money. The video, as far as the editing goes, was organic. When I first saw it, the first cut, I was like "what... the... fuck... did... we...just... do?" I was skeptical through the whole process. I was like, "We have something here, but I don't know if we have enough coverage." Once we put it all together, I was like "Oh my God. Are we going to put this shit on?" I was really doubting like "How crazy is this. Hey, this is what it's going to be. This is what we're going to do. We're going to cause a fucking ruckus." That was the get from the go. Look what happened!

MAZADI VISION, DIRECTOR:

We created a reaction from people. That's what we did. Was it a negative or a bad note? It's all the same. At the end of the day, those views really add up. The viewer is like, "Look at this piece of shit." And they're going to go show their friends. The one person who thought it was a piece of shit. The chances are that they're going to spread it to two other people saying "This is a piece of shit that I saw." It ends up working out better for us. Bad publicity is good publicity. That's definitely what happened here. Even the guys who didn't like it, it created a reaction. From the beginning we wanted people talking about this. We made it happen.

COUSINS:

SLIM JESUS: DRILL TIME

RICH BRIAN: DAT $TICK

STITCHES: MAIL

THE BRILLIANT YOUTUBE COMMENTS OF "BRICK IN YO FACE."

YouTube comments are bad. There is less trolling than you think these days. Most comments are things like "Who is still listening in 2017?" or "They should play this artist instead of Drake." "Brick In Yo Face" features high level roast comedy.

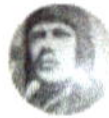

Ultraextreme 7 months ago
Mozart would be proud

321 REPLY

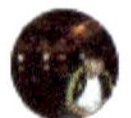

Calebmufcthompson 4 months ago (edited)
What a kind looking, well mannered group of gentleman

116 REPLY

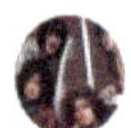

Bjorn- James Hanrahan 6 months ago
If you injected a pineapple with steroids and sprinkle coke on it and it became a person.

280 REPLY

Dylan Drake 1 year ago
Never has there been this much Florida in one man

1.9K REPLY

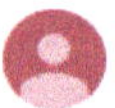

not creative enough for name 1 year ago
Billions of years of evolution for this

1.2K REPLY

This one is a joke, right?

miskee11 7 months ago
My dad would sing this randomly when I was younger. After he passed and we attended his funeral, my brother and I sang this and cried. Still love the song but sometimes it's hard to listen to.

389 REPLY

Right?[97]

97 Right?

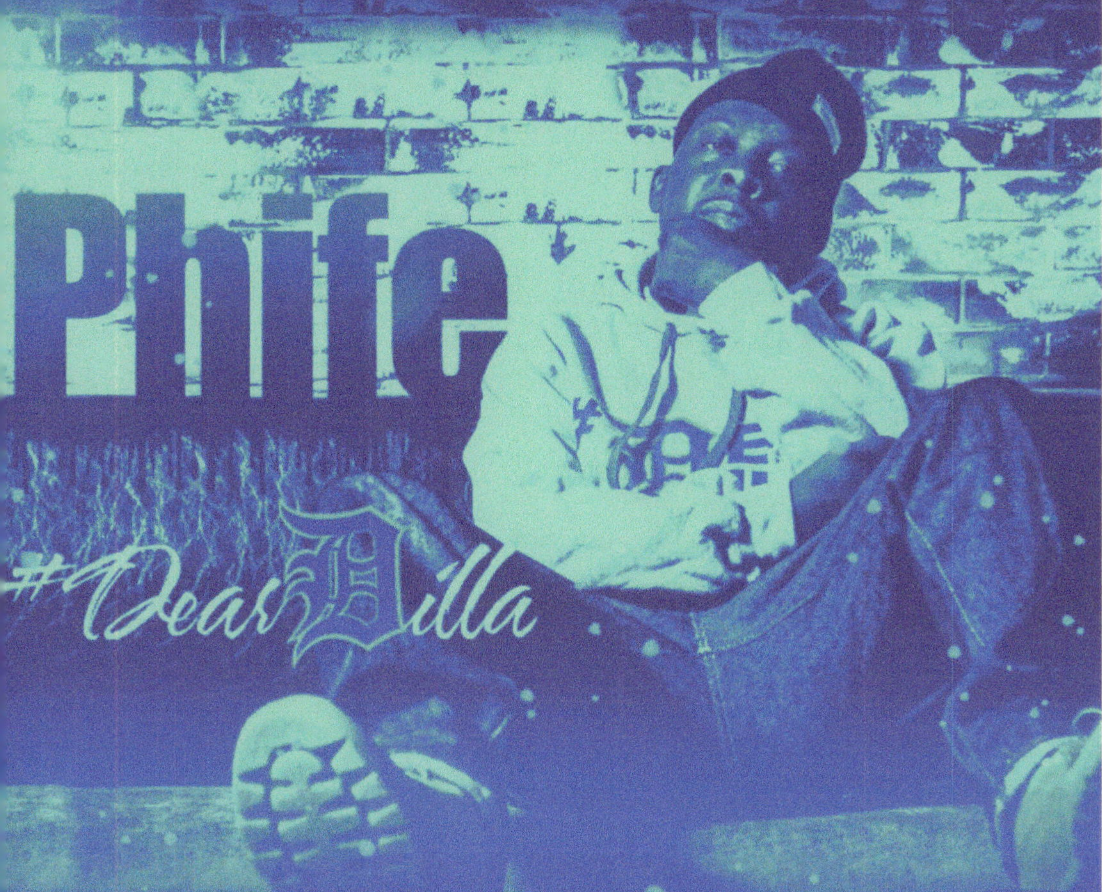

CHAPTER 10

PHIFE DAWG: DEAR DILLA

On "Dear Dilla," legendary A Tribe Called Quest emcee Phife Dawg warmly expresses that he misses his friend and collaborator J. Dilla, the legendary producer who passed away at the age of 32. The song and video were largely a collaboration between Phife, his friend and manager DJ Rasta Root[98], and talented animator and filmmaker Konee Rok.

DJ RASTA ROOT, PRODUCER/ACTOR:

I went to school at Gettysburg College in Pennsylvania. I graduated in 1993. In the interim, I was working in DC and DJing on the weekends. My school called me and said 'Tribe's[99] coming for a Spring Fling. They want to do some press. Would you come back to school being that you were on the radio station at Gettysburg College and do the interview?" I'm like, "Hell yeah." I had to rearrange some things. I had a gig that day. I didn't get to go to the concert but I went to the school. I was living in DC about an hour away. I interviewed Phife and Tip at the radio station. Ali wasn't there. We hung out. I have some video of it. I showed Phife before. He was like "I don't remember that at all." Tribe traveled so much, they've probably done a million interviews at a million colleges. So later that year, I got accepted to the JET[100] program to teach English in Japan. I'm Canadian, so I'm a Canadian JET. So I flew from Toronto. My family and I drove up for Caribana[101] and I didn't go because I was leaving that Saturday morning. The night before I left, Tribe was performing at Caribana in Toronto with Craig Mack.[102] That was like my last send off for hip-hop with me going to Japan for 3 years. About a year after I came back, it's like 1998, close to 99. My friend calls me and says "Phife is recording a song with us for one of the projects we're doing and we need some

---

98 By his associates, Dion Liverpool is interchangeably called DJ Rasta Root, Rasta Root, Rasta Roots, Root, and Roots. It seems fitting due to the number of hats he wears.

99 A Tribe Called Quest. In a unique twist, the group's name is always shortened to "Tribe" in spite of the fact that their name is instructing you to call them "Quest."

100 Japan Exchange and Teaching, a Japanese government initiative that brings college graduates to Japan to teach English language and athletic classes.

101 The Peeks Toronto Carribean Carnival, a celebration of Carribean culture.

102 After Bad Boy Records dropped B.I.G.'s *Ready to Die*, it dropped Mack's *Project Funk da World. PFdW*, featured the mega-hit Fehérlófia"Flava In Ya Ear" and "Get Down," both produced by the underappreciated Easy Mo Bee.

scratches. Would you like to come in and do the scratches?"[103] I'm like, "Yeah, sure." He absolutely had a DJ, but he had falling out with the DJ after they had broken up with Tribe. He was doing his solo stuff. I'm like "I'm going to go," being an ambitious young DJ. "I'm going to go to the studio and impress him." We hung out a little bit. My family is from Trinidad[104] so we kind of vibed off that. And I went about my business. The song never even came out, I don't think. About 6 months after that, I got a call from the same guy saying, "Hey, Phife asked me about you. He's looking for a DJ to do a show at the University of Maryland. He was wondering if you are available. And that's kind of how everything started."

From their trivial beginnings, Rasta Root and Phife would develop a relationship that became increasingly close. Rasta Root served as a manager, business partner, and collaborator to Phife. Rasta Root said that their relationship eventually settled at "best friends."

JORGE "JAY" SOTO, SPECIAL CONTRIBUTOR:

Me[105] and Roots go back years. We met during my freshman year in college. That's when I first met Phife and Roots. I was actually the opening act for when they came out to do a concert at my University. Then, our relationship blossomed over the years. Everytime Phife and Roots would come into town, they would reach out to me. We started to hang. Basically, we became family. We met back in 2001 or 2002. I've been in the music industry for years. I started in the hip hop industry and then I moved over the Latin industry. Then I started working behind the scenes. Whenever they were in town, we were always doing something together, whether it was me attending a show or us going out to dinner.

---

103 I fancy myself as sort of an internet sleuth. When DJ Rasta Root told me this, I didn't follow up as I knew that I could track this release down using my power of being a nerd. When I couldn't figure this out, I emailed Roots with my tail between my legs to clarify. I was able to sign in relief when he told me that the record never came out.

104 Phife often shouted out his Trini heritage. From *Oh My God:* "Trini gladiator. Anti-hesitator. Shaheed push the fader. From here to Grenada."

105 Jay Soto, also known as NorthRock, is the Co-Founder of NorthRock 360. If you are a science teacher, you may want to incorporate his "Trip to Outer Space" into your curriculum.

HERMAN "UNCLE HERM" HAYES, ACTOR/LOCATION SCOUT[106]:

In 2005, J was in the hospital before he even went into that last tour. And I'm the food and beverage director down at the Buckhead Courtyard here in Atlanta. I was moving around a little bit. And so I did the banquet for the Alliance of Lupus Research and a little lady came and thanked me. My service was on point and I was on everything. The food was good, the service was good, and we got to talking. I was like, "Well, you know I'd like to donate something because my nephew has lupus. He's in the hospital in California. And I like to come to one of your walks." So that was maybe October 2015. Then, he died in February but I had moved to another hotel. And so I went back and dug in that Rolodex and I got Mrs. Chapman's number. I called her and I was like, "I want to come to one of your walks next year and I want to make a donation." So for two months, man, this lady, she probably went and dug up to see who Dilla was and started calling me like every other day. "You should do a walk." I was like, "Look, lady. I have never done one, I'm from the hood. I don't know nothing about raising money for walks. I don't want to be associated with misappropriating funds."

That's how I ended up doing a lupus walk. So first, my very first lupus walk, I'm standing in front of the Tabernacle. I don't know if you know of the Tabernacle. It's a concert venue in Atlanta. So A Tribe Called Quest is there. That's a Friday night. Talib Kweli is with them on his Eardrum Tour. I'm standing in front of the Tabernacle passing out these fliers. So a white boy walked past with a *Donuts*[107] shirt on and I just picked him out. I was like, "Hey. Come here!" And he was like, "What?" and I was like, "Here's a flier. You need to be at this walk. And this kid, his name is Dillon. Dillon Vaughan Maurer[108] and he's the dopest rapper, intelligent, wordsmith kid which I had no idea when I was calling him. I just thought he was a kid coming to the show.

So, I'm talking to Dillon and he posted a photo and he's like, "Are you really J. Dilla's uncle?" I was

---

106 Herman Hayes is the brother of J. Dilla's mother, Maureen Yancey, commonly known in the hip-hop world as Ma Dukes.

107 Dilla recorded *Donuts,* an album consisting of short instrumental pieces in the final months of his life. Released only three days before his passing, it is widely considered to be classic.

108 Dillon Maurer, performs as Dillon. I first encountered his work with Paten Locke. Their track with Cool Calm Pete, "Rosie Perez" is a favorite and its video is one of my Low Budget Classics. A heartwarming aside to this story is that Herm and Dillon have remained very close through the years. Herm calls him "one of my closest confidants to this day." He also describes that Dillon and Phife were the creators of Uncle Herm "because during this time, I'm Herman Hayes that works for Marriott My nephew's name, James Yancey, nobody knows who the fuck I am."

like, "Yeah, I am." And he just fucking starts shaking and sweating, and he grabbed my hand and he started fucking bowing. I was like, "Hey! What the fuck are you doing?" He was like, "You don't understand. He was a god." He's talking about my nephew, and like I say, I don't know about this "beat god" shit.

Then, Rasta Root walks past me and then he comes asking... well, the motherfucker, he walked past me like two times. He walked close and then stopped and asked me. He was like, "Are you really J Dilla's uncle?" I was like, "Would I be out here in front of A Tribe Called Quest concert passing out fliers saying I'm Dilla's uncle if I wasn't?" He kind of looked. He's like, "I'm going to go talk to Tip[109]." I'm like, "I don't give a fuck who you're going to talk to."

But I continue to pass out fliers and he comes back. I was like, "This guy is irritable." I was thinking he's going to tell me I can't stand here and pass out the fliers. This is the feeling that I'm getting. So he comes and he was like, "Oh, you want to come with me?" I was like, "Where?" He's like, "I'm going backstage." I was like, "For what?" He's like, "I want to introduce you to Q-Tip and Tribe." And I was like, "No, I'm good."

And he was like, "What do you mean?" I was like, "I'm trying to pass out…" Because you see, I'm from Detroit. We straight hood, I'm finna hit all these windshields once everyone goes inside. Then, I'm going to take my ass home, you know and get ready for the lupus walk the next day.

So he's like, "No, man, I will take you…" and he'd asked me a couple times and I was like, "Yeah, okay. But I'm coming back to my spot." So he takes me in and introduces me. The first person he kind of passed me off, not really introduced me but the first person we saw was Jarobi.[110] And he said, "Hey Jarobi, come here. This is J. Dilla's uncle."

Puffy was there. You know the whole crew, everybody was flocked into Atlanta for Tribe. What the fuck? With Kweli? Come on. That's a dope show.

And, so [Rasta] Root went on to take care of business and run. He's running around anyway when he first saw me. So it's kind of weird that he had asked and stopped to say, "Are you really…" and to

109 Q-Tip. Because this takes place in ATL, I find it necessary to distinguish between Q-Tip and T.I., originally known as T.I.P.

110 Jarobi is a member of A Tribe Called Quest. Many diehard ATCQ fans don't know him for good reason. After being instrumental to the group's founding and debut album, Jarobi pursued a career as a chef. On the group's most recent album, *We Got It From Here...Thank You 4 Your Service,* he resumed a crucial role, contributing vocals to seven songs.

come back and take me inside. Because I can see the brother was running around. He has all kinds of paperwork in his arms and he is rushing. Plus, he had to DJ.

A SUPERFLUOUS DILLA STORY COURTESY OF UNCLE HERM

Herman "Uncle Herm" Hayes, Actor/Location Scout: Let me tell you just a quick story. So I had a little medical transportation we call, back in the '90s, it's called Luxe Med.

I pull a stopover to go get my mom one day. I'm not picking up customers. I mean my mom's at my sister's house, so I go get her. So James is there, comes out. It was a Ford van that was leathered out, had a TV on each seat in the back. So each person can watch their own TV. You know flip the thing down and there was a TV there with headphones and all kinds of shit. And he was like, "Oh, you can pick my people up, man, at the airport." And I was like, "Man, this ain't for rock stars and shit." And I'm like, "This is a fucking... see that handicap sticker? I just don't have a wheelchair lift in this one." My intentions were to buy one with a wheelchair lift, you know. For at the time, I was just taking people who could actually get in the van with walkers and stuff like that.

But he was like, "Oh man, can you pick up my..." I was like, "Man, I'm picking up handicapped people." So as he's leaving out of the van, he was like, "I know you bumpin' my stuff in here." I was like, "Man, I'm on some different shit." So him being a smartass kid. Like I said, that was our relationship with how close we were. Because of the donuts, he wasn't so much of a recluse with me as he was with other people, you know.

So I was like, "No, man." I'm like, "J, you know I'm on some different stuff?" So he pops it out, ejects the CD outside, pushes it back in and smiles. I think nothing of it.

I was like, yeah, he probably is making a smartass. So, now this was in the '90s. This was '98, '99 maybe. You know what I mean, probably '98. And he didn't say anything. I did not realize until I'm at his service in 2006, the one we had in Detroit. And we had obituaries made with his discography on it. And I'm scrolling down through it while I'm at the fucking service memorial, and I stop and I look and I see Brand New Heavies. And that was the CD that I had that he popped out, The Brand New Heavies *Saturday Nite*.

And I said, "Motherfucker" – I'm at the church and I just looked up like, "You motherfucker!" Never ever said a fucking word. He gave me that smirk, that smirking little smile. And he stepped down in my van. "See you, Unc!"

I was progressing to rap. So I'm listening to stuff like the Brand New Heavies with jazz bass going into hip hop, you know. And just didn't have no idea that that was his shit, man that he wouldn't tell – he told me after he died.

So it's kind of crazy. I finally went in. Jarobi took me over to meet [Ali Shaheed] Muhammad. So you know how Muhammad is? Almost a carbon copy of Dilla. They just don't look alike: the persona, the laid backness, the genuine nice guy shit. Incredible young man.

Then I met Q-Tip. Me and Tip talked for a minute. You know he said, "I remember coming to Detroit, to your sister's house." I was like, "Yeah. I think I missed you. I came right after you all left." And shit like that. And you know we all talked and we took a picture and then I'm standing backstage when, boom! I see this little black motherfucker, peeking and coming towards us and mean mugging. I'm like, "Who is this motherfucker?" I'm not sure if it's Phife because I don't watch all the videos. I'm not in that world.

So I'm thinking now that it must be Phife. But then when he got close, I was like, "What is happening" because Phife ran his hands around me like a metal detector. He didn't say a fucking word, but just stopped and froze and got close to me. And I was like, "This motherfucker high as hell. He ain't ready to go on stage. He fucked up." But then he stopped in there. His hands went to a hug. It was just like verifying, you know, scanning me. Something about him and Dilla was mystical and magical.

I didn't know Phife before J died.

KONEE ROK, DIRECTOR:

I first met Phife in Los Angeles on the Bounce tour. I was on the road with Rhymefest[111] and he was opening for A Tribe Called Quest.[112]. I think that was 2006. I remember being backstage after the show. The whole crew was there. Jarobi. Ali Shaheed Muhammad. I interviewed Q-Tip. Michael Rapaport and Leonardo Dicaprio[113] were there too. I met DJ Rasta Root[114] (Roots), who was Phife's manager and A Tribe Called Quest's road manager. Fast forward five years later. So I'm part of a B-boy crew called Chicago Tribe. One of the members from my crew, who goes by the

111 Rhymefest, a very talented rapper in his own right, has won three Grammy Awards for co-writing Kanye West's hits "Jesus Walks" and "New Slaves" as well as the John Legend/Common collaboration "Glory." I would highly recommend that you track down some of his independent collaborations. Personal favorites include the Molemen tracks "How We Chill" and "Keep The Fame."

112 Rhymefest opened for A Tribe Called Quest on 9/10/2006 at the Wiltern in Los Angeles.

113 An actor famous for appearing on popular 80s and 90s sitcom *Growing Pains.*

114 DJ Rasta Root is commonly known as "Roots."

name of Check-It, is a promoter as well and throws competitions, battles. He was collaborating with Jon Huang, who throws a lot of concerts in Chicago. They were putting together a show at Puma, where Phife was the headliner. They brought me in to film that and make a little piece about the show. I interviewed Phife, documented the battle, the concert, everything. We're at the venue called The Mid.[115] At the end of the night, it's late, close to 2 am. I'm just sitting backstage with my camera and my camera bag. I notice Phife is just sitting back there too, hanging out. Roots was there too. I thought to myself, "I wonder what Phife's working on these days? I wonder if he's doing any music on his own, because I don't think A Tribe Called Quest is making new stuff." I was going to leave. I was going to say something to him as I was leaving and ask him. But as I was about to go talk to him, someone started talking to him. It seemed awkward to interrupt him, so I was like "It's all good. I'm just going to go. I don't wanna interrupt the conversation." So then I left the venue and I was going home and realized, "I forgot my camera bag! The whole reason I was there." I went back inside and found my bag. Thank goodness. And Phife was just sitting there, the person he was talking to was gone. So, I said, "What's up, how's it going? You working on any new stuff these days?" He was like, "Yeah, I'm actually working on some new music." Keep in mind that we're shouting because of the music. He told me to pass my contact stuff to Rasta Root. Roots was right there and we exchanged numbers.

DJ RASTA ROOT, PRODUCER/ACTOR:

I go off of vibes. He had a good vibe. I kind of talked to Phife for a little bit and he said "Let's talk to him'"

KONEE ROK, DIRECTOR:

I left the club and I think even on the ride home, we were communicating. Right away they were sending me music, instrumentals, ideas, beats. Right away there was a chemistry. We were vibing through email and text. They kept sending me different concepts that they were planning and I kept sending ideas I would do. We did that for a year or two, just simmering.

115 306 N. Halsted Street, Chicago.

DJ RASTA ROOT, PRODUCER/ACTOR:

We spoke to him and the ideas that he had off-topic without even having a song. He had really creative ideas. As we started coming up with the "Dear Dilla" song, we started letting him hear parts of it. I gave him the lyrics and he was able to start working on a treatment for it. His treatments aren't normal. They're animated treatments.[116]

SUPERFLUOUS DILLA STORY #2

Herman "Uncle Herm" Hayes, Actor/Location Scout: I never called him Dilla. I mean I always call Dilla "James." I mean everybody in my family, it was James. So we got a friend rapper, Supa Emcee[117], you know. He's from Detroit and I knew him as a baby. One of my middle sisters, under Maureen, was friends with his auntie and they live in Virginia. So I knew him as a baby. When he's coming up, he liked rapping. And my sister, Rita was like, "Oh, my nephew, he's a producer and wants..." Supa Emcee, then a teenager says, "Oh yeah, what's his name?" and my sister said, "James".

So we... fast-forward about 10 years later, he's like, "Man, let me tell you something. I met your sister, Rita." And he told me the story and he was like, "She didn't tell me that was Dilla. She just says some n---- named James." And he says, "It blew my mind when I finally found out it was Dilla." And he said he called his mom and told them, "Call Aunt Rita." He's like, "Why didn't you tell me it was this?" [Rita] was like, "I didn't even know he was Dilla." You know what I mean?

KONEE ROK, DIRECTOR:

One day Roots sent me the instrumental to *Dear Dilla* that he produced. "Yo we're thinking about this." I said "Sounds cool." Little bit after that, they sent me a version with the lyrics and said "Can you put together a treatment for this?" I took a few days to do it, maybe a week. I wrote a paragraph and drew one image. The image was the title *Dear Dilla* on the top, and on the left hand was a hospital room with a curtain divider. On one side was Phife sick in the hospital with a sports magazine on his belly. On the left side was Dilla with all his instruments and his music and his

---

116 It can't be stated enough how dope Konee Rok's animated treatments are. Check out a side-by-side shot of what Konee planned for *Dear Dilla* by searching for "Pre-visualization of Phife Dawg's "Dear Dilla" Music Video" on Vimeo.

117 A member of the Guilty Simpson affiliated crew Almighty Dreadnaughtz.

records all over his hospital bed and his wheelchair making music on his bed. They really liked it and said "Can you draw storyboards?" I put that together and they liked everything. They were like "Word, what's the next step?" We had a phone call. We talked about the cost and the logistics and they immediately booked a flight to shoot in Chicago. I planned on shooting part of it in Chicago and part of it in Detroit. My team was here. My cinematographer, Jason 'DJ Intel' Deuchler, he shoots 80% of the music videos I direct.

JASON "DJ INTEL" DEUCHLER, CINEMATOGRAPHER:

I've known Konee back since he was a b-boy break dancer and I was a DJ back in high school. I've known him forever and he was the guy who always had a camera and I always had my camcorder also. I'd always do recording all these b-boy events and live concerts. Then eventually Konee started doing a documentary about Chicago hip-hop and I gave him all my tapes. We went to Columbia College together briefly for a little bit and kicked it off from there. The first product we work together on was it was a Rhymefest music video, *Stolen*, that was pretty successful. We've been working together ever since.

UNCLE HERM DIGGING STORY

Herman "Uncle Herm" Hayes, Actor/Location Scout: Dilla was like the only kid in my car that would actually want to get out of the car when I was buying new records. I wasn't crate digging. I was buying new records. I would get my check, go get my bag of weed. My next stop was to go to the record store. Dilla was the only kid who wanted to get out of the fucking car. "Can I go in?" and I'm like, "Okay. Yeah, yeah, you want to go in?" I mean, so this kid was digging – 6, 7, 8, 9 years old and looking and reading the back of every album in my mom's house. You know like a fiend, like a nerd that wants to read books. He would come in and hit the floor and read the albums. Our relationship was just heavy.

One notable thing about Konee is that he's very good at storyboarding. He came at me with a pretty solid concept in what he was looking for image-wise. We went through his overall design and added my input to it.

JORGE "JAY" SOTO, SPECIAL CONTRIBUTOR:

Roots reached out to me and said "I have this idea. I've been talking to Konee. I've been getting with him on a creative level. I think he's really dope. We're going to film this video and since it's your city, I think it would be really dope if you took part in it." I'm like "I'm in. If it's for Phife. I'll do anything for Phife." He is one of the more genuine people I've ever met in my life. It was a no-brainer.

KONEE ROK, DIRECTOR:

There were a lot of practical reasons to shoot [in Chicago]. Phife was coming from somewhere in the Bay Area. Roots lived in Atlanta. And J. Dilla and those aspects were in Detroit. They booked a flight and I had 30 days to organize, plan all the shots, get all of the locations, and think up every aspect of the video. I think they booked it for November 18th, 2013. It must have been October and truthfully, that was one of the hardest months of my life. There were a lot of personal reasons it was important to me, from my appreciation for the history of who Phife is. As well as this project being quintessential to the type of music video I want to do. So I wanted to nail it. And push it as far as I could. I was scouting locations. One scene, we're in a hospital room and I'm trying to find a hospital room. It's hard to get permission to shoot in a hospital. It wasn't happening. It ended up coming down to me converting the downstairs of my house into a hospital room. I needed a hospital bed. It is not easy to get a hospital bed. That is one of the hardest things I've ever done in my life. I ended up getting one from some guy in Milwaukee. He drove down and I might have paid him $300 and bought a hospital bed from him. I had to get a dialysis machine because I wanted to portray Phife fighting his diabetes. I went on a special trip to pick one up in a far-off Chicago suburb. It was dark and I went with Root's friend NorthRock. Let's just say that anyone who owns a used dialysis machine and is holding onto it, you can do your own math about that person!

It was really hard but we were able to do it. It wasn't just about getting a hospital bed. It was about portraying the look that we were going for. We were trying to get it correct. I think that ended up working out. We were able to get a hold of a venue downtown in Chicago, American Junkie[118] courtesy of the venue manager/friend DJ Chris Mix. He was really cool about using that spot for the concert setting in the video. They came in on a Thursday night, November 17th, and we planned to shoot the whole concert scene on Friday. We put out a casting call to get extras for the concert.

---

118 American Junkie, 15 W. Illinois St, Chicago. Closed.

It was real-life Phife fans who came out for the concert. We had a whole film crew that Intel and I put together. Jonathan Young was on the lights. Joel McGinty operated the crane and did a great job. My wife Nicole and her sister Jenny helped out a lot. To make it happen I think we shot all day. Ali Shaheed Muhammad flew in last minute to play Phife's doctor. We used a kitchen at the venue for the doctors office. For the concert scene, my b-boy crew, Chicago Tribe, also came out. I thought it was fitting that I met Phife at a battle thrown by my crew and they ended up getting to be in the video. . I think that's kind of interesting. After we shot, we had to go to my house to shoot the hospital scene. I think we ended up shooting until 3 or 4 a.m. I don't even know if we went to sleep. DJ Intel actually had to go spin a DJ gig while we were shooting. He left and came back and we were **still** shooting. As soon as we finished shooting at my house, about 10 of us jumped into a Winnebago and headed to Detroit.

JORGE "JAY" SOTO, SPECIAL CONTRIBUTOR:

So Konee and I are spearheading getting together all of this stuff for the music video. The dialysis machine is just supposed to be in the background. Where the hell are we going to get a kidney dialysis machine? So he starts looking up where the hell you can find it. He was scouring the internet. He finds an ad online, I think it was on Craigslist for a used kidney dialysis machine. I'm like, "for real bro?" He's like "Yah dude, can we go get it?" At that time, he didn't have a vehicle. So he's like "can we just jump in your car?" And I was like, "Alright, dude." I'm thinking, "How bad can it be?" I have a '99 Toyota Corolla. So I was like, "All right." First things first, we set up this trip to pick up this damn kidney dialysis machine. I'm like, "Where is it?" I don't remember if it was in Westchester[119], but it was far. It was in the boonies. It was some country part of Illinois, lots of trees, long drive. We get to this house and he goes and he meets the guy. He's telling me, "The guy is kind of eccentric, maybe a little different. He's not the most comforting kind of guy." His spidey sense is going off a little bit. So all of a sudden he escorts us to the house. This guy wanted to invite us to have a drink, have food, talk. He needed that social interaction. It's cool. *(Offering excuses to the seller)* 'We just got to get back to the city. We have a long drive.' He shows us this damn kidney dialysis machine. First off, it looked like something out of an old creepy murderer movie. First off, WHY? Why do you have a functioning kidney dialysis machine in your garage? I said, "Konee, you made this deal. This is on you. Just make sure you're back in five minutes. Because if you're not, I know how those movies go *(laughing)*. I'm a Puerto Rican dude. You're a white dude. You're probably going to be the first to die." He takes us to see this damn kidney dialysis machine.

---

119 Westchester, Illinois is roughly 30 minutes outside of Chicago with no traffic.

I'm like, "Holy shit. This thing's enormous." It was monstrously heavy. He's like, "Yeah, we got it!" I'm like, "This thing's not going to fit in my car. There's absolutely no way this big-ass, kidney dialysis machine is going to fit inside my old, four door, champagne, '99 Toyota Corolla. This is not going to happen." Konee is like, "Nah nah nah, we'll be cool." Konee, of course with his optimistic personality. We literally spent a good forty-five minutes to an hour just trying to develop a plan on how to fit it into the car. We lowered seats. We put seats back. We put them forward. We ended up laying the passenger seat completely down and rolling down the windows so that we could manipulate our arms through it. We somehow manage to slide this thing through the backseat into the front seat, laying it down with the seat in the full recline position. I'm like, "Fuck dude. My interior is getting scratched up." He's like, "don't worry about it." Everything is getting banged up. I'm like, "this is terrible."

JORGE "JAY" SOTO, SPECIAL CONTRIBUTOR:

We finally manage to squeeze it in the passenger side. I see Konee and I'm like, "Where the hell are you going to sit?" Literally, this man squeezes behind the driver's side on the back seat so we could ride home. Now, the weight of this thing was out of this world. It was ridiculously heavy. All of the tubes looked dirty as hell like somebody had still used it. I'm like, "Is someone giving someone a lobotomy with this thing?" The funny thing was it wasn't until we were driving back, we're like, (excitedly) "We've got this machine!" Konee looks at me like, "Is this thing even legal to have? This is legit medical equipment. I'm not sure if we're even supposed to have this." He's like, "Yeah... hmmmmmmm." We get back to the house. We unload it. We put it inside the garage temporarily. But this thing is as old as old gets, and it's so creepy. I don't even know how many stories that thing has. I just want to say a prayer. Just for that damn thing sitting in the corner of the garage.

JASON "DJ INTEL" DEUCHLER, CINEMATOGRAPHER:

The biggest challenge for the Detroit part of the video was we started in Chicago. We got in an RV, drove to Detroit, shot all day long, and drove back. The biggest challenge was getting 8 people into a 6-person RV driving to Detroit after shooting all day long.

JORGE "JAY" SOTO, SPECIAL CONTRIBUTOR:

We filmed a lot of the video in Detroit. I remember myself, my brother, and Roots drove to pick up this damn RV, this huge enormous RV. Roots was not thinking about where it was going to be parked or anything. We ended up parking it in front of my brother's house for the night, over by

O'Hare. We pick it up the next morning. We were just going to drive. We're like, "Who's going to drive?" Roots was like, "I figure you could drive, your brother could drive, I could drive." I've never driven one of these big ass things before. It was enough space to somewhat function. If you were to ask who got the most sleep on that trip, of course the answer would be Phife. He had the whole back bedroom to himself. There was a small little shelf, a sleeping area off the cockpit of the RV. That's where Konee was with his wife. She was assisting on the shoot as well. He was up there with her. Intel's getting on one sofa.

KONEE ROK, DIRECTOR:

I climbed onto the top bunk of the Winnebago, starting backing up all the footage from the shoot thus far. Then took a nap as we drove six hours to Detroit.

JORGE "JAY" SOTO, SPECIAL CONTRIBUTOR:

We're Puerto Rican and we're from Humboldt Park. When don't we bicker? You watch people on the Jersey Shore? It's like watching two strong-minded brothers from the neighborhood of Humboldt Park. If we weren't fighting, it wasn't normal. We were fighting the whole way there. We argued about driving. We argued about food. My brother ended up having an asthma attack while he was driving the bus at two or three in the morning. We were arguing about that because I didn't know what the hell was going on. He's like, "I can't breathe. Fuckin' asthma." I'm like, "Do you want me to drive?" "No, I got it." "Well then stop complaining. If you're okay, stop complaining. If you're not okay, then I'll drive." "No, I'm fine." "Then stop complaining." Things like that. At first, it was really rough for Phife to see that. He didn't understand the dynamic. But after he knew us for so many years, he was like, "I want to take you guys on tour. You guys are hilarious. This is the highlight of my trip. Watching you guys bicker. Who needs television? I've got the Soto Brothers."

JASON "DJ INTEL" DEUCHLER, CINEMATOGRAPHER:

On either the drive up there or the drive back, I totally passed out sleeping sitting in the chair. I'm looking like my eyes are totally open, but I'm asleep. Phife took video of it and roasted me. First off, that's like, "Wow, that's hilarious." But then, it's like "Holy crap. Phife Dawg's making fun of me."

JORGE "JAY" SOTO, SPECIAL CONTRIBUTOR:

There was another guy who was there too, but I don't recall him, his name. I wasn't very fond of the guy. It's Phife, he's a very easygoing dude. Except when you start talking about sports. Then he wants to argue about everything. I brought my Xbox on the road with us so we can play. Phife liked video games. We all liked video games. All of us play sports games. It's different if you don't know Phife. If you know Phife, you can have the dynamic with him where you can banter back and forth and argue. We used to argue all the time about sports. That was our thing. If you don't know Phife, and you are new to a situation, and you're working, you shouldn't really be cursing at the main artist on the bus over a video game. Needless to say, that was an interesting experience with old boy. I wish him nothing but the best.

SOME OTHER CHICAGO/DETROIT CONNECTIONS

Dwele+Kanye "Hold On," Dennis Rodman, Doug Collins, Bison Dele, John Salley, Brad Sellers, Orlando Woolridge, Ben Wallace, Lindsay Hunter, Ben Gordon, Magglio Ordoñez, Rudy York, Rocky Colavito, Eddie Cicotte, Freddy Garcia, David Wells, Al Albuquerque, Kyle Farnsworth, Austin Jackson, Edwin Jackson, Howard Johnson, Neifi Perez, Rondell White, a bunch of Kanye and Big Sean collabs, Slum Village f/ Kanye's "Selfish," Joique Bell, Dick Jauron, Erik Kramer, Route 94.

KONEE ROK, DIRECTOR:

We got to Detroit, jumped out, and we started shooting right away at the location.

JASON "DJ INTEL" DEUCHLER, CINEMATOGRAPHER:

I knew we were shooting in Detroit, so I wanted to make sure Detroit came off as a great city as it is. People always focus on the depressing side of Detroit, so we made a point to keep everything vibrant and colorful to celebrate life through celebrating Dilla.

KONEE ROK, DIRECTOR:

A week before, we hired someone who worked out there to shoot with us. Intel and I scouted, got some shots, and then Uncle Herm, J.Dilla's uncle, took us everywhere and he even gave us some Dilla's Delights' donuts. It was awesome. So when we ended up going there with Phife, we were ready to go. We knew what to do. We had it sketched out.

HERMAN "UNCLE HERM" HAYES, ACTOR/LOCATION SCOUT:

Phife is the only constituent of Dilla's, that would ask about the girls[120] every time he came to Detroit or saw me or saw Ma Dukes. It was such a genuine friendship that he and I had, which is a whole 'nother book chapter of our meeting and our friendship. He had Rasta Roots call me because he was going through some dialysis at the time. Phife was up and down that last year. He was being so strong. I said "What do you need me to do?" All the video shoots, I showed him where to go. With the signs, with the "Welcome to Detroit." On top of the building where the donut shop is.[121] The whole building was vacant at the time and I was the caregiver of the building. I gave up my job working at the bakery. So I told the racist company[122] that owns the building, 'I'll go from being a bakery manager making that good money. I'll take that $9 an hour to watch your building." I'm talking about a 200 room hotel. That building was totally empty when we shot the video. Upstairs was in the shots around the building. Comerica was right next door to the shop. That's how close I am to the ballpark.

KONEE ROK, DIRECTOR:

Uncle Herm was preparing to open a donut shop as a tribute to J. Dilla called Dilla's Delights.

---

120 J. Dilla's daughters

121 Dilla's Delights was located in the historic Milner Hotel.

122 Uncle Herm has faced a great deal of obstacles in his attempts to open a donut shop in memory of his legendary nephew. Foremost, Dilla's Delights has not enjoyed unwavering support from their landlords. Uncle Herm: "It's a ten story apartment building now that was the historic Milner Hotel. Ma Dukes and Mr. Yancey ran a little restaurant in that building. It was important and epic that I got that spot. That was November of 2014 when we shot that. We didn't open until May of 2016. We were being gentrified out at the time of the video. I signed my lease in January of 2013. From the end of 2013 through the middle of 2014, people started coming in downtown Detroit and buying out the buildings. The square footage was going through the roof. The people who gave me the lease were trying to get rid of me. I was going to bake my donuts there in the basement and use upstairs and flip it over to retail every morning around 4 o'clock so we could open at 6. Due to the gentrification and blocking me out, they took my basement space away. They left me with only 450 feet of retail space upstairs. I helped open a bakery called Avalon Breads that had grown quite a bit since then. [Avalon] offered to give me production space. They thought I was going to back out since I couldn't make my donuts there. I said 'Okay, I got a place to make them, which is not even a mile from the downtown spot and I'll just use it for retail.' I continued to make them until we closed in March. I got a lot of dirt on them. They did a lot of stupid stuff like working against the historic building codes, because it is a historic Detroit building."
"I got my place but that's just a minute part of what my life is about. Avalon gave me the space. I got it open. They probably still hate me to this day. My lease is up in February of 2021. They ended up giving me a 5 year lease. They took it away from me and gave me a 2 year lease. Then when I got the dirt on them, they gave me the 5 year lease back. In 2016, my lease went to 2021 of February."

The treatment was written with the idea that the donut shop would be open by the time we were ready to shoot the video. But the location wasn't ready yet. We had to pretend it was open during the shoot, crossing our fingers that it would be open by the time the video was released. Dwele[123] ended up showing up playing the chef in the scene in the restaurant where Roots is enjoying a delicious breakfast and Phife is quote-unquote enjoying some cantaloupe.

The shot in front of the shop when we're not even open yet. It was Amp Fiddler, myself, Brian[124], Dwele. We were all standing in front with Phife. There was a break in there. We were out there talking and chatting. Phife hadn't seen Amp Fiddler since he handed Q-Tip the Slum Village tape on the bus back in the day. Before Tip and J got together. He gave him a Slum Vill tape with J beats on it and some Slum Village shit. Phife had not seen Amp since that day. When Konee got there, he was like "I need a cameo." I was like "Okay." I had already set everything up.

When we shot out front, there was a pause and Phife said "Come on in." We went inside. He said "Are you okay?" I said "Yeah, but motherfuckers are trying to take this shit. They don't want us to have this." We're in the middle of the entertainment district and they don't understand who Dilla is or what it means for the city to have something Dilla downtown. It wasn't their clique. They weren't gonna get it and they still don't get it.

And he grabbed my hand and we prayed.. And that was horrible. There was nothing straight in there. It was still a construction and stuff like that. And when I went in, he locked the door, and we started having our discussion. We just stood there and prayed, man. He's like, "It's going to happen, Herm. It's going to happen."

With Dilla's Delights not officially open, Konee Rok employed some creative tricks to fool the viewer. I don't care to admit how long it took me to notice that the donut shop's signs were added digitally.

HERMAN "UNCLE HERM" HAYES, ACTOR/LOCATION SCOUT:

I set up the video shoot. I set everything up basically. I set up the video shoot in the restaurant around the corner with Dwele and Phife and Rasta Root.. It was in Al's Mediterranean but now, it's Jose's Mexican.

123 Even if you don't know Dwele, you know Dwele. He lends vocals to Kanye West's "Power" and "Flashing Lights." His "Hold On (Remix)" with Kanye is on my list of favorite songs.

124 Brian "Cryzko" DeBois.

Throughout Dear Dilla, the video highlights Phife's complicated relationship with food. Phife is encouraged to make good choices through this journey by those who love him, including Dwele, Ali Shaheed Muhammad, and DJ Rasta Root. Root and Phife have real comedic chemistry.

DJ RASTA ROOT, PRODUCER/ACTOR:

I did elementary theater and then for my senior year in college, I did a two-man play. Me and another guy. We did a play but that's it. I had stage fright, honestly. I don't like to talk in front of people, but we have a natural jokey chemistry. It wasn't hard to do that.

DEAR X RAP SONGS

DOPE

2Pac: Dear Mama. Pac writes one of rap's most heartfelt songs. Because of my love of rap videos, whenever I hear this, I picture his mom spreading peanut butter on bread.

Masta Ace: Dear Diary. Rap pioneer Ace ponders whether his rap career may be ending. Ironically, the song is so dope that it extends his career infinitely. Impressive sampling of the Moody Blues by producer Domingo.

Jay-Z: Dear Summer. In either a marketing ploy or an amazing act of friendship, "retired" Jay-Z drops the summer classic on the album of lablemate and friend Memphis Bleek. I lived in NYC at the time and this song was definitely top dog for a couple of months.

Phife: Dear Dilla. Rap royalty's ode to rap royalty.

WORST CAREER DECISION EVER

Sole: Dear Elpee. Sole, then making waves as key member of indy label Anticon, disses indy legend El-P, then a member of legendary Company Flow. El-P and Sole have a phone conversation and Sole, when confronted, says "I said I love Company Flow... I don't wanna be against you guys... I wanna be down." El-P records the call and makes it the backbone of retort "Linda Tripp."

DJ RASTA ROOT, PRODUCER/ACTOR:

That was Konee's idea. All the stuff with the food, the donut, shaking head was Konee. The bike with the candy bar was Konee. He had a vision, I think. He had some other ideas that we kind of shot down. Those were the ones that stuck, you know.

HERMAN "UNCLE HERM" HAYES, ACTOR/LOCATION SCOUT:

I brought the donuts. I had maybe two, three dozen donuts, some to eat during the day, some for the last final video shoot of Phife and the bakery and me rolling out the dough. Standing there with Rasta Root. There was supposed to be three donuts left by the end of the day for the final shoot. So that was like 8:00, 9:00 in the morning, but we didn't finish that last shot until probably 9:30, 10:00 at night because we're going all over the city.

So it's time to go to the Avalon Bakehouse for me to roll out dough to do the donut shot. Everybody pulls in and it was just like, "Where's the fucking donuts?" And all the donuts are gone out of the box on the van. So last minute ditch, Amy and Mike Vanover ran out to find donuts for the last video shoot in the dark and in the rain. So those donuts in the last shot when Phife has taken a bite out of a donut and Rasta Root says, "No," those are not Dilla's Delights. Those are from Detroit Donuts in Hamtramck[125], Michigan because they ate all the donuts that were on the bus, and some were supposed to be saved for the video shoot. So I didn't have time. I'm just faking rolling dough. That wasn't even donut dough. I think I grabbed some bread dough from the stollen. I would say, "Kurt, give me some dough so I can be rolling it out for the video shoot." You know what I mean? But yeah, that donut was not my donut.

HERMAN "UNCLE HERM" HAYES, ACTOR/LOCATION SCOUT:

Amy and Mike were so helpful on the shoot all day. We rolled around. It was crazy. Mike's truck, the windshield wiper went out.

I set up down on Melodies & Memories and then we shot with Dilla's girls and Phife and me. So we're in front of Melodies & Memories and the girls are there, having a good reunion. Phife took a bunch of pictures with the girls, a bunch of silly pictures that are not in the shoot. Phife is licking out his tongue at everybody else because he's got Dilla's girls in his arms.

But the day of the video shoot, all the stuff that was inside. It was raining. We got a little gap that morning for Phife to take pictures and stuff in front of Melodies & Memories. But for the most part, while we were filming inside the restaurant, it was pouring down. We got a little break for Phife and Rasta Root to shoot riding the bicycle down to the street next to the donut shop. And

---

125 Hamtramck, named Best City Name Ever by me, is located fully within Detroit like Eswatini is located fully within South Africa. Now would be a fair moment for you to admit that you learned that Swaziland changed its name to Eswatini from a book about rap videos.

then a slight rain when we were taking the pictures in front of the shop. But for the most part, the rest of the day is raining like crazy.

But we made it happen. Like I say, I was really busy, I was running around. I'm satisfied. I was exhausted, but we work like that every day, 16 hours to 20 hours a day for the last four or five years. Even a couple years before the shop was opened, I'm riding around with my bicycle, sampling donuts, telling people it's coming. You know I got some business cards that say "Opening in Fall of 2013" and we didn't open until three years later.

KONEE ROK, DIRECTOR:

Basically, we shot from Thursday night, shot Friday all day into the A.M. on Saturday. We drove to Detroit, shot all day there and came back in the A.M. on Sunday. Then, I shot extra stuff here with just me and Intel. We went out and got the rest of the shots we needed to finish the video. We had to shoot an airplane and the marquee outside of a concert venue. Then we were done. We shot non-stop for like 3 days, got it done, and they left. I finished editing by mid-December. Then I moved on to the animation sequences in Tribe Called Quest colors[126] of J. Dilla making beats. I was done working on the video by my birthday on December 21st.

HERMAN "UNCLE HERM" HAYES, ACTOR/LOCATION SCOUT:

We filmed some a day before the main shoot because it was sunny. The film in front of Maureen, my sister, in front of her house, was shot the previous day.

DJ RASTA ROOT, PRODUCER/ACTOR:

The animations, oh my God! So much so that a year after it came out, I got a call from the Smithsonian and they were honoring Dilla. They looked online for Dilla songs that embody him and they took Dear Dilla, the hook part where it shows the drum machines. Crazy! It's an interactive display. They have it on the 4th floor and it shows a drum machine and you tap it.

JASON "DJ INTEL" DEUCHLER, CINEMATOGRAPHER:

The animation portion with the Tribe Low End Theory colors with Dilla doing the beat pads on the end of his hospital bed. That's actually Konee's wife sitting on a chair. We filmed her and Konee

126 A Tribe Called Quest albums featured very distinctive art, typically featuring red, green, white and sometimes yellow on a black background.

animated over that. That was cool, to see that come-to-life animation from a practical element. We shot it as basically an FX plate with Konee's wife sitting in, and went back and animated it.

KONEE ROK, DIRECTOR:

The animation was all day, every day for two weeks. The closing credits and the 10 to 12 second sequence in the middle, those are like a couple of weeks of work. We were playing off of the samples. Roots did such a great job of producing the song. There are a lot of details there that I wanted to accentuate because they all had meaning. Dilla's catalogue. I wanted to visualize that. I really cared about the details. I wanted to put in some Easter Eggs and give it a lot of substance. I wanted it to be thick and rich with things that people would care about; people that love A Tribe Called Quest, people that love Dilla. I wanted it to be full of what was nourishing for those people.

DONUTS

Herman "Uncle Herm" Hayes, Actor/Location Scout: I'm 65 years old so I've been through this a million times over. The whole Dilla thing is weird. It didn't start until my 50's. I mean me and J had a good relationship. I mean, I'm 'The Donut Guy.'

I'm the guy who gave him his first fucking donut. You know what I mean? I worked for a company called Dawn Donuts, and J was a little boy and I used to bring his dad donuts. And the dad asked me one day, "What happened to the donuts?" I was like, "I left them on the kitchen table" and Dewitt called me and said, "I found the box." He said, "It was under James' bed, crushed in the corner."

So he smashed them. Honest, recluse kid that stole donuts one day and I was like, "You only need to say and tell me when you want a fucking donut." And he used to bug the shit out of me. I was like, "Man, you won't even fucking talk to people and you're fucking bugging me. How about you leave me alone?" "Give me some donuts. Give me some donuts." He would not disappear or leave like half a foot from me until I was like, "Okay, Saturday. Damn! Leave me alone."

People are not making trendy music with trendy titles and verbs on their deathbed. You got a beat album with titles telling you a life story; telling you "bye," telling you "don't cry," telling you "this is my last fucking donut tonight," you know?

DJ RASTA ROOT, PRODUCER/ACTOR:

We shot different cuts of it. If I can remember, he had a clearly animated storyboard and he followed it to a T. It was just a matter of seeing what we had been talking about for months come to life on the RED[127] cameras that we were using.

Once we wrapped it up I'm the type of person where I don't want to do anything that's regular or mundane. When Konee Rock first did the eye blinking at the beginning of the credits in the Tribe[128] colors, he used this really gooshy, slimy noise. It felt creepy. We ended up using pages turning in a book. Little details like that. We really worked as a team to get it done.

JASON "DJ INTEL" DEUCHLER, CINEMATOGRAPHER:

Konee figured out the shot where Phife has all his clothes just fall off him. It looks like it was kind of a stop animation type of thing but we actually did it and shot it in reverse. That's actually really happening, just it's backward.

JORGE "JAY" SOTO, SPECIAL CONTRIBUTOR:

Konee was just determined to make that music video. Everything. When I say "everything," I just mean "everything." He used his entire imagination to create this spectacle. Even now, when I watch the video, I have to laugh because it looks so legit. If you were to break down footage scene-by-scene, the opening sequence where you see Phife laying in the bed, do you know where that was? That was inside the house, the downstairs of the house. It was his living room. Same thing with the scene with the silhouette of Dilla behind the curtain. That was his creativity on how it was going to be shot. At first, I couldn't see the vision. But as I watched the music video, you can't even tell where that was shot. The doctor scene where Phife is speaking to the doctor, the pretty doctor with the glasses. That wasn't a doctor's office. That was the office of a bar[129], the bar that we used for the music video that doesn't even exist anymore. The level of creativity was "plus-ten."

---

127 RED Digital Cinema was an early innovator of digital cameras, creating a camera that could rival film without the high cost of film. Peter Jackson was an early adopter, using to shoot the short film *Crossing The Line*. Upon seeing it, Steven Soderbergh said "I have to shoot with this."

128 A Tribe Called Quest

129 The aforementioned American Junkie.

DJ RASTA ROOT, PRODUCER/ACTOR:

This was a labor of love if you think of it. We took the bus and went out to Detroit. We had a time crunch in general. They filmed Slum Village. They filmed the B-roll stuff and the background stuff for the scenes in Detroit. We made sure to include his two daughters, even though at the time the daughters' mothers weren't on talking terms. I had to play mediator and say literally "This is **not** about you guys doing something for your daughter's father, and they have to be in the video. His mom has to be in the video. You'd be remiss if you left them out."

JASON "DJ INTEL" DEUCHLER, CINEMATOGRAPHER:

It was cool meeting Ma Dukes and Dilla's family, his two daughters and his Uncle Herm. That was such an honor, and a really cool thing was just being in Detroit, and it was really, really cool. It was a blessing to be able to work with everyone.

JORGE "JAY" SOTO, SPECIAL CONTRIBUTOR:

The Detroit part was really dope, too, because we actually went to Dilla's crib, went to the record store. We went to see Uncle Herm actually make donuts.

DJ RASTA ROOT, PRODUCER/ACTOR:

We also shot his Uncle Herm and Amp Fiddler[130], who kind of taught Dilla to produce. While I was in it, all these people impacted Dilla's life, and he impacted their life. Shaheed[131] was in there at the end. Something that was weird was the nurse we hired. The actor who played the nurse had actually received a kidney donation.[132] We found her on Craigslist. These little things made it more special.

From top to bottom, we treated it like we had an unlimited budget, but we didn't. We paid for it ourselves. Konee Rok did a lot of the stuff pro bono out of the love of the project, which was amazing. But there were a lot of inherent costs that we took care of: camera rental, venue rental, the

---

130 Amp Fiddler mentored a young J.Dilla. As evidence of his appreciation and loyalty, Dilla frequently gave Amp Fiddler BANGER beats. Feel free to check out "Through Your Soul" as evidence.

131 Ali Shaheed Muhammed, founding member of A Tribe Called Quest and Lucy Pearl. Along with Q-Tip and Dilla, formed the legendary production trio The Ummah.

132 Notable as Phife received a kidney transplant from his wife in 2008. Kidney failure also contributed to the death of J. Dilla in 2006.

van. We took an RV from Chicago to Detroit. We shot in Chicago the next morning, got up, went to Detroit, shot that day and that night came back.

JASON "DJ INTEL" DEUCHLER, CINEMATOGRAPHER:

It was basically like a 72-hour shoot. We sort of just pushed. It was long but it was pretty much a smooth shoot. Everyone was in good spirits. Timing and things like that can sort of get you down.

KONEE ROK, DIRECTOR:

Roots did something special. He organized a movie premiere the weekend of J. Dilla's birthday, premiering it before anyone saw it online. We showed it at the theater. It was awesome. Great release party. We did a panel discussion and people asked questions. We showed it and the crowd wanted to see it again so we showed it twice. They even printed out movie posters and we got to sign them for people. It was a great night.

DJ RASTA ROOT, PRODUCER/ACTOR:

When that was done, I said "We really have to release this song in a way no one ever had before. We found a theater here. Some sponsors ended up renting a theater with 250 seats in Atlanta, and we did like a release of the video. We invited 250 people: press, tastemakers and whatever. We showed the video, and had a Q&A. We had healthy food choices for the sponsors, coconut water for the drinks. When we released it in Atlanta, it was a big thing. People were like "Why didn't I think about showing my 3 minute video in a two-hour block at a movie theater?" It was kind of crazy. We had Phife there, me, the director, 4-Ize who played Dilla in the wheelchair. It was a very big moment for marketing number one, and number two, certainly for the Hip Hop scene in Atlanta. We turned around the next day and flew to Detroit for Dilla Day and showed the video there, and Phife performed there. Everything was special. I knew it couldn't be regular.

KONEE ROK, DIRECTOR:

Right after the premier, we hopped on a plane and went to Detroit for Dilla Day[133] because it was the next day. We went to Dilla Day and showed the video there. And we released it, it came out on TV; VH1 MTV Centric. Then, it came out online. People seemed to enjoy it. All of us that were a

133 Dilla Day, a commemoration of Dilla's birthday, is celebrated by fans worldwide. Prominent locations, like Dilla's hometown of Detroit, often have official events. On 2/7/14, fans who attended Detroit's Fillmore, shown in the video, were lucky to see frequent Dilla collaborators De La Soul, Slum Village, Phat Kat, and Guilty Simpson. Also, DJ Premier and Pete Rock battled. Who won? Fans of music.

part of it were really proud of it. It might be my favorite project that I've ever done.

JORGE "JAY" SOTO, SPECIAL CONTRIBUTOR:

That was the first time Konee and I got together to work. I say work but in reality this was all fun to me. If I could do that every day for the rest of my life that would be amazing. There was an instant chemistry. He's a great, great dude. His ideas. His vision. The things that we did to make that music video happen are some of the fondest memories I'll ever hold.

JASON "DJ INTEL" DEUCHLER, CINEMATOGRAPHER:

There weren't too many challenges. Getting people scheduled appropriately was a little bit tough because there were so many cameos. For the most part, I was very happy how it worked out.

JORGE "JAY" SOTO, SPECIAL CONTRIBUTOR:

American Junkie, I ran that whole thing. I was the primary contact for it, scheduling all of the extras, for the performance scene, getting them all to location on time. I was the stand-in on stage for Phife. We drove to Detroit to help set up. I was the one who got the make-up artist. He actually drove with us to Detroit. All of us had our own parts to make it work. But Konee was the creative genius behind it. Konee and Roots. And of course, Phife digging the whole idea.

DJ RASTA ROOT, PRODUCER/ACTOR:

Phife liked it a lot. He was skeptical at first. Being vulnerable in a hospital bed was a reality for him with the illness and stuff. I totally give him props for opening up and letting the world see this side of him. The scene where he's on the side of the stage and he almost doesn't want to perform. That's very real. There were times where he would be puking, ill. One time, the elevation in Denver was affecting him. It was very personal but only if you knew what he really went through, you wouldn't think it was artistic liberty. It was very real. I don't think the dream part was real. I think they took artistic liberty with that, but Dilla was always in his day to day.

Uncle Herm had an emotional response upon first seeing the video.

HERMAN "UNCLE HERM" HAYES, ACTOR/LOCATION SCOUT:

Tears. Absolutely. Absolutely. I was watching it with somebody and you know how proud we men are, I had to dash out in this, you know. And like, fuck! I mean it was such a beautiful thing. Like I say, being a part of it and watching it put together like that. I don't think I first-time I watched, I saw the shots with me. When it came on with the shot in the hospital, I was just like, "Oh he's just going to shock us, right? I was naturally honored to be a part of it.

Dear Dilla has always contained bittersweet tones. In spite of its humor and celebration, its viewers were forced to confront the loss of the legendary J. Dilla.[134] On March 22, 2016, Phife Dawg passed away at 45 years old. Dear Dilla became a video in which a tragically passed hip-hop legend mourns his friend, another tragically passed hip-hop legend. While Konee Rok and Rasta Root agreed on the direction of "Dear Dilla," they disagree on whether Phife was motivated by his approaching mortality.

KONEE ROK, DIRECTOR:

It's definitely bittersweet. You've got nostalgia, music history, all this love, and all these people that are his fam. This family element going on. I don't know exactly what was going on with Phife in particular but we all knew his health wasn't great. I don't know what he thought. If he wasn't sure about how long he would be around. The nature of the song, the fact that they really put such an effort into getting this done. It seemed to me almost like he knew in a way. He might have known that he might not be here much longer. It was like foresight in a way. It was already so meaningful when it came out, and when he passed it was like it magnified the sentiment of it. The melancholy of it, a little bit solemn. It's not just another music video. It's not even a mini-movie. It's like a capsule of history, family, and music. It encapsulates so many elements. Definitely, it can never be emulated.

DJ RASTA ROOT, PRODUCER/ACTOR:

It's very poetic. That came out in 2014. He passed away two years after. It's "Hold tight, this is the last time I see you" and then actually wrote that line which is crazy. I started that first for him. I said, "Let's flip the Tip line, where he says 'Hold Tight.'" It was so real. It just makes it all the more crazy.

Not at that point. Because I think at that point, that was 2014. I'm trying to think where we were with that. 2008 was around the time the kidney his wife donated started failing. I think he was off dialysis. I don't think he understood the impact of the record. He was very adamant about finishing the album. He was lively, so it wasn't like a goodbye to the world. It was more like "Hey, I miss my

---

134 J. Dilla passed tragically at the age of 32. Media outlets have reported a variety of contributing ailments. A study of his production discography can make you doubt that he did so much in so short of a time. Pharcyde, Slum Village, A Tribe Called Quest, Jaylib, *Donuts, Like Water for Chocolate, Electric Circus, Ruff Draft, Welcome 2 Detroit, Amplified,* and countless hits for De La Soul, Busta, Erykah Badu, The Roots, Phat Kat, and other Detroit artists.

friend." When Dilla passed, it struck him hard and I kind of had to beg him, "This is your friend who passed away. Go to the funeral." He was only in Oakland and it happened in LA and so it wasn't too far to travel. I was like "Just go. It's important. Trust me." And he went and it wasn't a typical funeral. It was a party, you know?

COUSINS

AVERY*SUNSHINE: SCENARIO: I GOT SUNSHINE

PRE-VISUALIZATION OF PHIFE DAWG'S "DEAR DILLA" MUSIC VIDEO

A TRIBE CALLED QUEST: SCENARIO

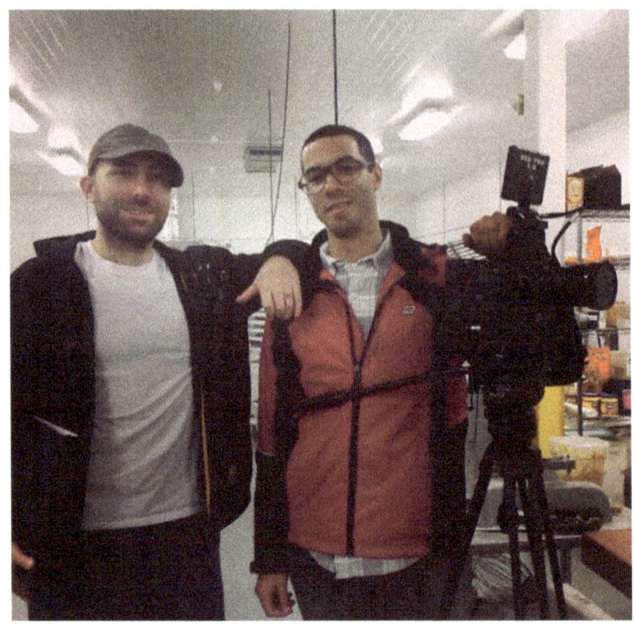

Konee Rok and DJ Intel on set. Photo courtesy of Konee Rok.

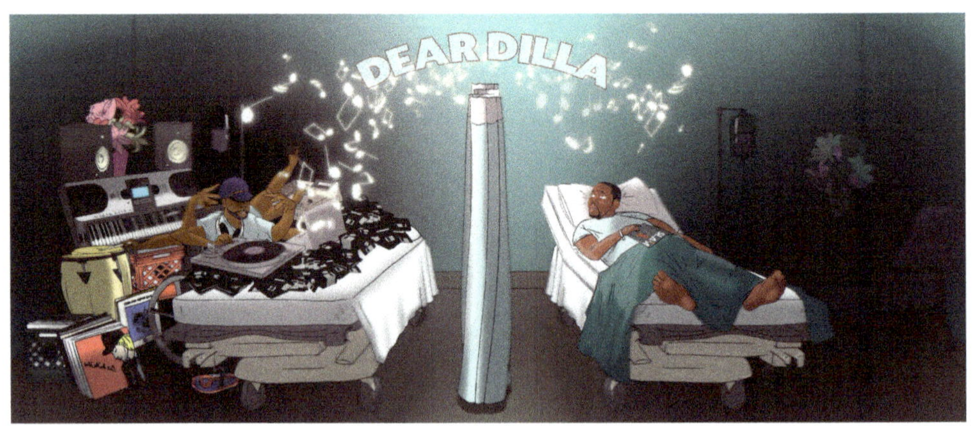

'Dear Dilla' treatment, by Konee Rok

Dear Dilla Breakdown by Konee Rok.

PHIFE - "DEAR DILLA" - MUSIC VIDEO
SHOT LIST/STORYBOARD BREAKDOWN

WRITER/EDITOR/DIRECTOR: KONEE ROK
CINEMATOGRAPHY/LIGHTING: JASON "INTEL" DEUCHLER
LIGHTING: JONATHAN YOUNG

SHOT #	VISUAL REFERENCE	CHARACTERS	WARDROAB	SETS	OBJECTS	FX	LIGHTING	TONE	CAMERA	NOTES
2A		PHIFE	GOWN	HOSPITAL ROOM	-PILLOW	X	DIM	DIS-ORIENTATION	STILL. VERY CLOSE.	PHIFE AWAKES. OBSERVES FLOWERS IN FRONT OF HIM. THEN DILLA BEHIND CURTAIN TO RIGHT. ONLY EYE MOVEMENT.
2B		PHIFE	GOWN	HOSPITAL ROOM	-PILLOW	X	DIM	DIS-ORIENTATION	STILL. VERY CLOSE.	PHIFE AWAKES. OBSERVES FLOWERS IN FRONT OF HIM. THEN DILLA BEHIND CURTAIN TO RIGHT. ONLY EYE MOVEMENT.
2C		PHIFE	GOWN	HOSPITAL ROOM	-PILLOW	X	DIM	DIS-ORIENTATION	STILL. VERY CLOSE.	PHIFE AWAKES. OBSERVES FLOWERS IN FRONT OF HIM. THEN DILLA BEHIND CURTAIN TO RIGHT. ONLY EYE MOVEMENT.
4A		PHIFE	GOWN	HOSPITAL ROOM	-PILLOW -BED	X	DIM	MELANCHOLY	STILL. CLOSE.	PHIFE NOTICES DILLA THEN GLANCES UP TO TV ABOVE.
4B		PHIFE	GOWN	HOSPITAL ROOM	-PILLOW -BED	X	DIM	MELANCHOLY	STILL. CLOSE.	PHIFE NOTICES DILLA THEN GLANCES UP TO TV ABOVE.

SHOT #	VISUAL REFERENCE	CHARACTERS	WARDROAB	SETS	OBJECTS	FX	LIGHTING	TONE	CAMERA	NOTES
7		PHIFE	-GOWN -WRIST NAME TAG	HOSPITAL ROOM	-PILLOW -BED	X	DIM	FRUSTRATION	STILL. CLOSE.	PHIFE PUTS HAND ON FACE IN DIRECT REACTION TO THE GAME AS WELL AS HIS SITUATION.
12A		PHIFE	-GOWN -WRIST NAME TAG	HOSPITAL ROOM	-PILLOW -BED	BLUE LIGHT	-DIM -BLUE LUMINANCE	MYSTERIOUS	STILL. CLOSE.	HAND STILL ON FACE. NOTICING LIGHT AND MUSIC. REMOVES HAND AND LOOKS AT CURTAIN TO HIS RIGHT.
12B		PHIFE	-GOWN -WRIST NAME TAG	HOSPITAL ROOM	-PILLOW -BED	BLUE LIGHT	-DIM -BLUE LUMINANCE	MYSTERIOUS	STILL. CLOSE.	HAND STILL ON FACE. NOTICING LIGHT AND MUSIC. REMOVES HAND AND LOOKS AT CURTAIN TO HIS RIGHT.
13		PHIFE	-GOWN -WRIST NAME TAG	HOSPITAL ROOM	-PILLOW -BED -CURTAIN -CHAIR -TABLE -FLOWERS -IV STAND	BLUE LIGHT	-DIM -BLUE LUMINANCE	MYSTERIOUS	SLIDE LEFT. WIDE.	PHIFE LOOKS RIGHT. CURIOUS AND CONFUSED BY THE MUSIC AND LIGHT.
14A		PHIFE	-GOWN	HOSPITAL ROOM	-PILLOW -BED	BLUE LIGHT	-DIM -BLUE LUMINANCE	MYSTERIOUS	STILL. CLOSE.	PHIFE LOOKS FROM UPABOVE CURTAIN TO DOWN AT DILLA'S FEET.
14B		PHIFE	-GOWN	HOSPITAL ROOM	-PILLOW -BED	BLUE LIGHT	-DIM -BLUE LUMINANCE	MYSTERIOUS	STILL. CLOSE.	PHIFE LOOKS FROM UPABOVE CURTAIN TO DOWN AT DILLA'S FEET.

SHOT #	VISUAL REFERENCE	CHARACTERS	WARDROAB	SETS	OBJECTS	FX	LIGHTING	TONE	CAMERA	NOTES
16		-DILLA - PHIFE	-GOWN -WRIST NAME TAG	HOSPITAL ROOM	-CURTAIN -BED	BLUE LIGHT	-DIM -BLUE LUMINANCE -SILHOUETTE	MYSTERIOUS	PULL IN. WIDE.	PHIFE SITS ON EDGEOF HIS BED WATCHING DILLA'S SIHLOUETTE NOD HIS HEAD WHILE BEATS .MAKING
17A		PHIFE	GOWN	HOSPITAL ROOM	-IV STAND	BLUE LIGHT	-DIM -BLUE LUMINANCE	MYSTERIOUS	STILL. MEDIUM CLOSE.	PHIFE IS UP FROM BED SLOWLY APPROACHING CURTAIN.
17B		PHIFE	GOWN	HOSPITAL ROOM	-IV STAND	BLUE LIGHT	-DIM -BLUE LUMINANCE	MYSTERIOUS	STILL. MEDIUM CLOSE.	PHIFE IS UP FROM BED SLOWLY APPROACHING CURTAIN.
18A		PHIFE	-GOWN -WRIST NAME TAG	HOSPITAL ROOM	-CURTAIN	BLUE LIGHT	-DIM -BLUE LUMINANCE	MYSTERIOUS	STILL	PHIFE SLOWLY PULLS OPEN CURTAIN.
18B		PHIFE	-GOWN -WRIST NAME TAG	HOSPITAL ROOM	-CURTAIN	BLUE LIGHT	-DIM -BLUE LUMINANCE	MYSTERIOUS	STILL	PHIFE SLOWLY PULLS OPEN CURTAIN.
19A		PHIFE	-GOWN -WRIST NAME TAG	HOSPITAL ROOM	-CURTAIN -BED	BLUE LIGHT	-DIM -BLUE LUMINANCE THAT FADES AWAY	OPTOMISM/D ISAPPOINTME NT	PULL OUT	PHIFE PULLS OPEN CURTAIN REVEALING A HAPPY FACE. HIS EXPRESSION TURNS TO DISAPPOINTMENT BLUE LIGHT FADES. CAMERA PULLS BACK REVEALS EMPTY BED.

SHOT #	VISUAL REFERENCE	CHARACTERS	WARDROAB	SETS	OBJECTS	FX	LIGHTING	TONE	CAMERA	NOTES
19B		PHIFE	-GOWN -WRIST NAME TAG	HOSPITAL ROOM	-CURTAIN -BED	BLUE LIGHT	-DIM -BLUE LUMINANCE THAT FADES AWAY	OPTOMISM/DISAPPOINTMENT	PULL OUT	PHIFE PULLS OPEN CURTAIN REVEALING A HAPPY FACE. HIS EXPRESSION TURNS TO DISAPPOINTMENT BLUE LIGHT FADES. CAMERA PULLS BACK REVEALS EMPTY BED.
19C		PHIFE	-GOWN -WRIST NAME TAG	HOSPITAL ROOM	-CURTAIN -BED	BLUE LIGHT	-DIM -BLUE LUMINANCE THAT FADES AWAY	OPTOMISM/DISAPPOINTMENT	PULL OUT	PHIFE PULLS OPEN CURTAIN REVEALING A HAPPY FACE. HIS EXPRESSION TURNS TO DISAPPOINTMENT BLUE LIGHT FADES. CAMERA PULLS BACK REVEALS EMPTY BED.
19D		PHIFE	-GOWN -WRIST NAME TAG	HOSPITAL ROOM	-CURTAIN -BED	BLUE LIGHT	-DIM -BLUE LUMINANCE THAT FADES AWAY	OPTOMISM/DISAPPOINTMENT	PULL OUT	PHIFE PULLS OPEN CURTAIN REVEALING A HAPPY FACE. HIS EXPRESSION TURNS TO DISAPPOINTMENT BLUE LIGHT FADES. CAMERA PULLS BACK REVEALS EMPTY BED.
19E		PHIFE	-GOWN -WRIST NAME TAG	HOSPITAL ROOM	-CURTAIN -BED	BLUE LIGHT	-DIM -BLUE LUMINANCE THAT FADES AWAY	OPTOMISM/DISAPPOINTMENT	PULL OUT	PHIFE PULLS OPEN CURTAIN REVEALING A HAPPY FACE. HIS EXPRESSION TURNS TO DISAPPOINTMENT BLUE LIGHT FADES. CAMERA PULLS BACK REVEALS EMPTY BED.
20A		PHIFE	-GOWN -WRIST NAME TAG	HOSPITAL ROOM	-PILLOW -BED	BED POPPING UP	-DARK	DETERMINATION	STILL. CLOSE.	PHIFE AWAKENS AND LITERALY POPS OUT OF HIS BED.

SHOT #	VISUAL REFERENCE	CHARACTERS	WARDROAB	SETS	OBJECTS	FX	LIGHTING	TONE	CAMERA	NOTES
20B	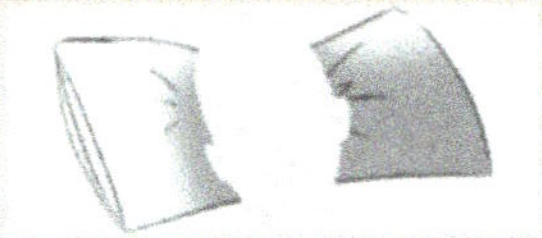	PHIFE	-GOWN -WRIST NAME TAG	HOSPITAL ROOM	-PILLOW -BED	BED POPPING UP	-DARK	DETERMINATI ON	STILL. CLOSE.	PHIFE AWAKENS AND LITERALY POPS OUT OF HIS BED.
20C		PHIFE	-GOWN -WRIST NAME TAG	HOSPITAL ROOM	-PILLOW -BED	BED POPPING UP	-DARK	DETERMINATI ON	STILL. CLOSE.	PHIFE AWAKENS AND LITERALY POPS OUT OF HIS BED.
21A		PHIFE	-GOWN -WRIST NAME TAG	HOSPITAL ROOM	-PILLOW -BED -CLOTHES	BED POPPING UP	-DARK	DEFIANCE	STILL .MEDIUM-WIDE.	PHIFE POPS OUT OF HIS BED AND HIS STREET CLOTHES FLY ONTO HIM.
21B	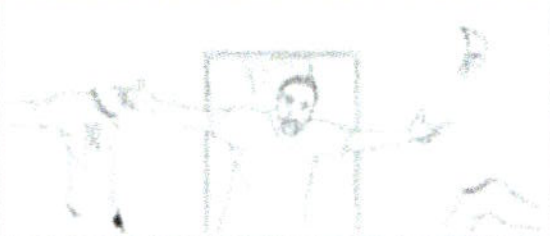	PHIFE	-GOWN -WRIST NAME TAG	HOSPITAL ROOM	-PILLOW -BED -CLOTHES	BED POPPING UP	-DARK TO BRIGHT	DEFIANCE	STILL. MEDIUM-WIDE.	PHIFE POPS OUT OF HIS BED AND HIS STREET CLOTHES FLY ONTO HIM.
21D	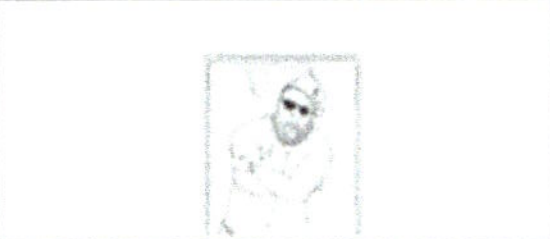	PHIFE	-SPORTY DETROIT JACKET -SUNGLASSES -HAT	HOSPITAL ROOM	-PILLOW -BED -CLOTHES	BED POPPING UP	BRIGHT	DEFIANCE	STILL. MEDIUM-WIDE.	PHIFE POPS OUT OF HIS BED AND HIS STREET CLOTHES FLY ONTO HIM.
22A	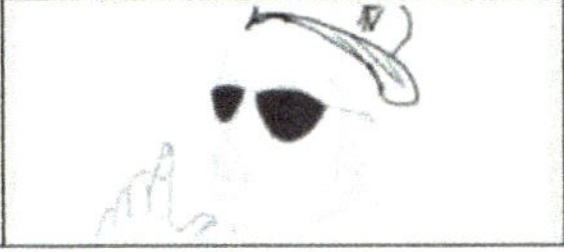	PHIFE	-SPORTY DETROIT JACKET -SUNGLASSES -HAT	HOSPITAL ROOM	X	X	BRIGHT	DEFIANCE	CLOSE. STILL THEN PAN UP	PERFORMANCE: "THAT'S MY WORD. I'MMA SEE YOU!" CAMERA GOES UP AND TRANSITIONS INTO DETROIT SKY.

SHOT #	VISUAL REFERENCE	CHARACTERS	WARDROAB	SETS	OBJECTS	FX	LIGHTING	TONE	CAMERA	NOTES
22B		PHIFE	-SPORTY DETROIT JACKET -SUNGLASSES -HAT	HOSPITAL ROOM	X	X	BRIGHT	DEFIANCE	CLOSE STILL THEN PAN UP	PERFORMANCE: "THAT'S MY WORD. I'MMA SEE YOU!" CAMERA GOES UP AND TRANSITIONS INTO DETROIT SKY.
26		PHIFE	-SPORTY DETROIT JACKET -SUNGLASSES -HAT	NEVADA SREET	X	X	DAYLIGHT	SENTIMENTAL	DOLLY BACK WITH HIS WALK. MEDIUM-WIDE.	PERFORMANCE: "I'MMA TELL YOU DILLA WHY THEY LACKING SKILLS PAL."
27A		-PHIFE -MA DUKES: MAUREEN YANCEY	-SPORTY DETROIT JACKET -SUNGLASSES -HAT	YANCEY HOME	DILLA CHILD PHOTO	X	DAYLIGHT	SENTIMENTAL	STILL. WIDE.	PERFORMANCE "NO STAGE PRESENCE, CADENCE, STYLE." PHIFE WALKS BY YANCEY FAMILY HOME. REVEALING MA DUKES STANDING IN FRONT WITH DILLA CHILDHOOD PICTURE.
27B		-PHIFE -MA DUKES: MAUREEN YANCEY	-SPORTY DETROIT JACKET -SUNGLASSES -HAT	YANCEY HOME	DILLA CHILD PHOTO	X	DAYLIGHT	SENTIMENTAL	STILL. WIDE.	PERFORMANCE "NO STAGE PRESENCE, CADENCE, STYLE." PHIFE WALKS BY YANCEY FAMILY HOME. REVEALING MA DUKES STANDING IN FRONT WITH DILLA CHILDHOOD PICTURE.
32		PHIFE	-SPORTY DETROIT JACKET -SUNGLASSES -HAT	SEVEN MILE STREET (HIP HOP SHOP)	X	X	DAYLIGHT	SENTIMENTAL	DOLLY BACK WITH HIS WALK	PERFORMANCE: "I REMINICE, REMINICE WHEN MOBB DROPPED SHOOK."

SHOT #	VISUAL REFERENCE	CHARACTERS	WARDROAB	SETS	OBJECTS	FX	LIGHTING	TONE	CAMERA	NOTES
33A		-PHIFE -DAUGHTERS: -JA'MYA -TY-MONAE	-SPORTY DETROIT JACKET -SUNGLASSES -HAT	RECORD STORE EXTERIOR	DILLA DJING PHOTO	X	DAYLIGHT	SENTIMENTAL	STILL	PERFORMANCE "SHAM WAS DOWN BY LAW" PHIFE WALKS BY RECORD STORE REVEALING DAUGHTERS STANDING IN FRONT WITH DILLA CHILDHOOD PICTURE.
33B		DAUGHTERS: -JA'MYA -TY-MONAE	UPPER CASUAL	RECORD STORE EXTERIOR	DILLA DJING PHOTO	X	DAYLIGHT	SENTIMENTAL	STILL. WIDE.	PERFORMANCE "SHAM WAS DOWN BY LAW SUCH A GOOD LOOK" PHIFE WALKS BY RECORD STORE REVEALING DAUGHTERS STANDING IN FRONT WITH DILLA CHILDHOOD
42		PHIFE	-SPORTY DETROIT JACKET -SUNGLASSES -HAT	DILLA'S DELIGHTS	X	X	DAYLIGHT	SENTIMENTAL	STILL. MEDIUM-CLOSE.	PERFORMANCE: "I'MMA THIRD OF THE TRIBE, BUT I'MMA SPEAK FOR THE CLICK."
43A		-PHIFE -GROUP	-SPORTY DETROIT JACKET -SUNGLASSES -HAT	DILLA'S DELIGHTS	X	X	DAYLIGHT	SENTIMENTAL	WIDE. STILL THEN TILT UP TO SKY AND HOLD	PERFORMANCE: "WHATTUPDO! WE MISS YOU KID!"
43B		-PHIFE -GROUP	-SPORTY DETROIT JACKET -SUNGLASSES -HAT	DILLA'S DELIGHTS	X	X	DAYLIGHT	SENTIMENTAL	STILL THEN TILT UP TO SKY AND HOLD	PERFORMANCE: "WHATTUPDO! WE MISS YOU KID!"

SHOT #	VISUAL REFERENCE	CHARACTERS	WARDROAB	SETS	OBJECTS	FX	LIGHTING	TONE	CAMERA	NOTES
43C		-PHIFE -GROUP	-SPORTY DETROIT JACKET -SUNGLASSES -HAT	DILLA'S DELIGHTS	X	X	DAYLIGHT	SENTIMENTAL	STILL THEN TILT UP TO SKY AND HOLD	PERFORMANCE: "WHATTUPDO! WE MISS YOU KID!" CAMERA TILTS UP TO THE CLOUDS AND TRANSITION INTO DILLA ANIMATED SEQUENCE
46		PHIFE	CASUAL	DILLA'S DELIGHTS	DONUT	X	EVENLY LIT ROOM LIGHTING	HUNGRY	STILL. PERSPECTIVE.	PHIFE HOLDS DONUT IN FRONT OF HIM.
47A		PHIFE	CASUAL	DILLA'S DELIGHTS	DONUT	X	EVENLY LIT ROOM LIGHTING	HUNGRY	STILL. MEDIUM-CLOSE	PHIFE EYES THE DONUT THEN BRINGS IT TOWARDS HIS MOUTH
47B		PHIFE	CASUAL	DILLA'S DELIGHTS	DONUT	X	EVENLY LIT ROOM LIGHTING	HUNGRY	STILL. MEDIUM-CLOSE	PHIFE STOPS AND LOOKS UP FROM DONUT
49A		PHIFE	CASUAL	DILLA'S DELIGHTS	DONUT	X	EVENLY LIT ROOM LIGHTING	FRUSTRATION	STILL. MEDIUM-CLOSE	PHIFE PAUSES THE STARES AT HIS DONUT COMPETITTIVELY.
49B		PHIFE	CASUAL	DILLA'S DELIGHTS	DONUT	X	EVENLY LIT ROOM LIGHTING	FRUSTRATION	STILL. MEDIUM-CLOSE	PHIFE PAUSES THE STARES AT HIS DONUT COMPETITTIVELY.

SHOT #	VISUAL REFERENCE	CHARACTERS	WARDROAB	SETS	OBJECTS	FX	LIGHTING	TONE	CAMERA	NOTES
50A		PHIFE	CASUAL	DILLA'S DELIGHTS	DONUT	GOING THROUGH DONUT HOLE	EVENLY LIT ROOM LIGHTING	FRUSTRATION	PULL INTO DONUT HOLE	TRANSITION THROUGH DONUT HOLE INTO EXAMINATION ROOM
50B		PHIFE	CASUAL	DILLA'S DELIGHTS	DONUT	GOING THROUGH DONUT HOLE	EVENLY LIT ROOM LIGHTING	FRUSTRATION	PULL INTO DONUT HOLE	TRANSITION THROUGH DONUT HOLE INTO EXAMINATION ROOM
50C		PHIFE	CASUAL	DILLA'S DELIGHTS	DONUT	GOING THROUGH DONUT HOLE	EVENLY LIT ROOM LIGHTING	FRUSTRATION	PULL INTO DONUT HOLE	TRANSITION THROUGH DONUT HOLE INTO EXAMINATION ROOM
52A		- PHIFE -DOCTOR	-GOWN -DOCTOR COAT	EXAM ROOM	-SCALE -CLIPBOARD	X	EVENLY LIT ROOM LIGHTING	APPROVAL?	STILL. MEDIUM. BACKGROUND PERSON OUT OF FOCUS.	PHIFE STAIRS AT SCALE
52B		-PHIFE -DOCTOR	-GOWN -DOCTOR COAT	EXAM ROOM	-SCALE -CLIPBOARD	X	EVENLY LIT ROOM LIGHTING	APPROVAL?	STILL. MEDIUM. PHIFE TURNS HEAD AND BACKGROUND PERSON NOW IN FOCUS.	PHIFE TURNS TO DOCTOR FOR APPROVAL. SHE SHAKES HER HEAD "NO".
52C		-PHIFE -DOCTOR	-GOWN -DOCTOR COAT	EXAM ROOM	-SCALE -CLIPBOARD	X	EVENLY LIT ROOM LIGHTING	APPROVAL?	STILL. MEDIUM. BACKGROUND PERSON BACK OUT OF FOCUS.	PHIFE TURNS BACK TO SCALE.

SHOT #	VISUAL REFERENCE	CHARACTERS	WARDROAB	SETS	OBJECTS	FX	LIGHTING	TONE	CAMERA	NOTES
52D		-PHIFE -DOCTOR	-GOWN -DOCTOR COAT	EXAM ROOM	-SCALE -CLIPBOARD	X	EVENLY LIT ROOM LIGHTING	APPROVAL?	STILL. MEDIUM.	PHIFE SHRUGS SHOULDERS.
53		-PHIFE -DOCTOR	-CASUAL -DOCTOR COAT	DOCTOR OFFICE	-KIDNEY CHART -PEN -MEDICAL POSTERS -DESK -2 CHAIRS	X	EVENLY LIT ROOM LIGHTING	CONCERN	STILL. WIDE.	DOCTOR EXPLAINS PHIFES CONDITION TO HIM USING KIDNEY MEDICAL CHART.
55A		-PHIFE -DOCTOR	-CASUAL -DOCTOR COAT	DOCTOR OFFICE	-KIDNEY CHART -PEN -MEDICAL POSTERS -DESK -2 CHAIRS	X	EVENLY LIT ROOM LIGHTING	CONCERN	HOLD ON DOC PAN RIGHT TO LEFT THEN HOLD ON PHIFE	DOCTORS FACE SERIOUS AS SHE EXPLAINS.
55B		-PHIFE -DOCTOR	-CASUAL -DOCTOR COAT	DOCTOR OFFICE	-KIDNEY CHART -PEN -MEDICAL POSTERS -DESK -2 CHAIRS	X	EVENLY LIT ROOM LIGHTING	CONCERN	HOLD ON DOC PAN RIGHT TO LEFT THEN HOLD ON PHIFE	DOCTORS FACE GOES TO CONCERNED AS CAMERA PANS TO PHIFE.
55C		-PHIFE -DOCTOR	-CASUAL -DOCTOR COAT	DOCTOR OFFICE	-KIDNEY CHART -PEN -MEDICAL POSTERS -DESK -2 CHAIRS	X	EVENLY LIT ROOM LIGHTING	CONCERN	HOLD ON DOC PAN RIGHT TO LEFT THEN HOLD ON PHIFE	DOCTORS FACE GOES TO CONCERNED AS CAMERA PANS TO PHIFE.
55D		-PHIFE -DOCTOR	-CASUAL -DOCTOR COAT	DOCTOR OFFICE	-KIDNEY CHART -PEN -MEDICAL POSTERS -DESK -2 CHAIRS	X	EVENLY LIT ROOM LIGHTING	CONCERN	HOLD ON DOC PAN RIGHT TO LEFT THEN HOLD ON PHIFE	PHIFE STARES BLANLY AT CHART.

SHOT #	VISUAL REFERENCE	CHARACTERS	WARDROAB	SETS	OBJECTS	FX	LIGHTING	TONE	CAMERA	NOTES
55E		-PHIFE -DOCTOR	-CASUAL -DOCTOR COAT	DOCTOR OFFICE	-KIDNEY CHART -PEN -MEDICAL POSTERS -DESK -2 CHAIRS	X	EVENLY LIT ROOM LIGHTING	CONCERN	HOLD ON DOC PAN RIGHT TO LEFT THEN HOLD ON PHIFE	DISSOLVE INTO JOGGING.
56A		PHIFE	JOGGING SUIT	CITY STREET	-IPOD EARBUDS	X	DAYLIGHT	STRUGGLE	DOLLYING BACK WITH HIS RUN HOLD ON FEET TILT UP TO HEAD & HOLD	PHIFE JOGGING.
56B		PHIFE	JOGGING SUIT	CITY STREET	-IPOD EARBUDS	X	DAYLIGHT	STRUGGLE	DOLLYING BACK WITH HIS RUN HOLD ON FEET TILT UP TO HEAD & HOLD	PHIFE JOGGING.
57		-PHIFE -RASTA ROOT	JOGGING SUIT	CITY STREET	-IPOD EARBUDS -SNICKERS -BIKE	X	DAYLIGHT	STRUGGLE	MEDIUM-WIDE. STILL WHILE DOLLYING BACK WITH HIS RUN	RASTA RIDES BIKE DANGLING SNICKERS IN FRONT OF PHIFE AS HE JOGS.
59A		-PHIFE -RASTA ROOT	CASUAL	DINER INTERIOR	-TABLE SETTING -HEARTY BREAKFAST -1 GRAPEFRUIT	X	EVENLY LIT ROOM LIGHTING	STRUGGLE	-FRAME -DOWN -FRAME -LEFT -FRAME -UP -FRAME	RASTA RECIEVES HIS PLATE OF FOOD WHICH IS NOTICEABLY APPETISING AND UNHEALTHY
59B		-PHIFE -RASTA ROOT	CASUAL	DINER INTERIOR	-TABLE SETTING -HEARTY BREAKFAST -1 GRAPEFRUIT	X	EVENLY LIT ROOM LIGHTING	STRUGGLE	-FRAME -DOWN -FRAME -LEFT -FRAME -UP -FRAME	RASTA RECIEVES HIS PLATE OF FOOD WHICH IS NOTICEABLY APPETISING AND UNHEALTHY

SHOT #	VISUAL REFERENCE	CHARACTERS	WARDROAB	SETS	OBJECTS	FX	LIGHTING	TONE	CAMERA	NOTES
59C		-PHIFE -RASTA ROOT	CASUAL	DINER INTERIOR	-TABLE SETTING -HEARTY BREAKFAST -1 GRAPEFRUIT	X	EVENLY LIT ROOM LIGHTING	STRUGGLE	-FRAME -DOWN -FRAME -LEFT -FRAME -UP -FRAME	RASTA RECIEVES HIS PLATE OF FOOD WHICH IS NOTICEABLY APPETISING AND UNHEALTHY
59D		-PHIFE -RASTA ROOT	CASUAL	DINER INTERIOR	-TABLE SETTING -HEARTY BREAKFAST -1 GRAPEFRUIT	X	EVENLY LIT ROOM LIGHTING	STRUGGLE	-FRAME -DOWN -FRAME -LEFT -FRAME -UP -FRAME	CAMERA MOVES FROM RASTA DELICIOUS PLATE TO PHIFES "HEALTHY" SINGLE SLICED GRAPEFRUIT PLATE.
59E		-PHIFE -RASTA ROOT	CASUAL	DINER INTERIOR	-TABLE SETTING -HEARTY BREAKFAST -1 GRAPEFRUIT	X	EVENLY LIT ROOM LIGHTING	STRUGGLE	-FRAME -DOWN -FRAME -LEFT -FRAME -UP -FRAME	CAMERA MOVES FROM RASTA DELICIOUS PLATE TO PHIFES "HEALTHY" SINGLE SLICED GRAPEFRUIT PLATE.
59F		-PHIFE -RASTA ROOT	CASUAL	DINER INTERIOR	-TABLE SETTING -HEARTY BREAKFAST -1 GRAPEFRUIT	X	EVENLY LIT ROOM LIGHTING	STRUGGLE	-FRAME -DOWN -FRAME -LEFT -FRAME -UP -FRAME	CAMERA MOVES UP FROM PHIFE'S PLATE TO HIS FACE.
59G		-PHIFE -RASTA ROOT	CASUAL	DINER INTERIOR	-TABLE SETTING -HEARTY BREAKFAST -1 GRAPEFRUIT	X	EVENLY LIT ROOM LIGHTING	STRUGGLE	-FRAME -DOWN -FRAME -LEFT -FRAME -UP -FRAME	PHIFE LOOKS UP AT RASTA.
59H		-PHIFE -RASTA ROOT	CASUAL	DINER INTERIOR	-TABLE SETTING -HEARTY BREAKFAST -1 GRAPEFRUIT	X	EVENLY LIT ROOM LIGHTING	STRUGGLE	-FRAME -DOWN -FRAME -LEFT -FRAME -UP -FRAME	PHIFE HAS HUMOURLESS EXPRESSION.

SHOT #	VISUAL REFERENCE	CHARACTERS	WARDROAB	SETS	OBJECTS	FX	LIGHTING	TONE	CAMERA	NOTES
64A	PHIFE DAWG	PHIFE	-SHOW GEAR -JACKET -HAT	BACK STAGE	-DRESSING ROOM SIGN -MIC	X	DIM	STRUGGLE	PULL OUT	PHIFE NAME ON GREEN ROOM DOOR IS AJAR.
64B		PHIFE	-SHOW GEAR -JACKET -HAT	BACK STAGE	-DRESSING ROOM SIGN -MIC	X	DIM	STRUGGLE	PULL OUT	CAM PULLS OUT TO REVEAL PHIFE LEANING OVER ON STAIRS. MIC IN HAND.
65A		PHIFE	-SHOW GEAR -JACKET -HAT	BACK STAGE STAIRS	-NEEDLES -VILES -DIALYSIS MACHINES	SUPER-IMPOSING FALLING OBJECTS	DIM	DIS-ORIENTATION	STILL	PHIFE LOOKS DIZZY SUPER-IMPOSED NEEDLES, VILES AND DIALYSIS MACHINES FALL IN FRONT OF HIM.
65B		PHIFE	-SHOW GEAR -JACKET -HAT	BACK STAGE STAIRS	-NEEDLES -VILES -DIALYSIS MACHINES	SUPER-IMPOSING FALLING OBJECTS	DIM	DIS-ORIENTATION	STILL	PHIFE LOOKS DIZZY SUPER-IMPOSED NEEDLES, VILES AND DIALYSIS MACHINES FALL IN FRONT OF HIM HAND COVERS FACE
67		PHIFE	-SHOW GEAR -JACKET -HAT	BACK STAGE STAIRS	-MIC	X	DIM	DEPRESSION	MEDIUM-CLOSE. SLOW SLIDE LEFT TO RIGHT	PHIFE NOT DOING WELL ON STAIRS.
69A		PHIFE	-SHOW GEAR -JACKET -HAT	BACK STAGE STAIRS	-MIC	X	DIM	WONDER	STILL	PHIFE'S HAND OVER FACE.

SHOT #	VISUAL REFERENCE	CHARACTERS	WARDROAB	SETS	OBJECTS	FX	LIGHTING	TONE	CAMERA	NOTES
69B		PHIFE	-SHOW GEAR -JACKET -HAT	BACK STAGE STAIRS	-MIC	X	DIM	WONDER	STILL	HE REMOVES HAND AND LOOKS UP STAIRS.
72A		PHIFE	-SHOW GEAR -JACKET -HAT	BACK STAGE STAIRS	X	X	DIM	DETERMINATI ON	STILL	PHIFE IS LOOKING UP THE STARES CURIOUSLY
72B		PHIFE	-SHOW GEAR -JACKET -HAT	BACK STAGE STAIRS	X	X	DIM	DETERMINATI ON	STILL	HE BEGINS TO WALK UP STAIRS
77A		PHIFE	-SHOW GEAR -JACKET -HAT	BACK STAGE	-CURTAIN	BLUE BACKLIGHT	DIM	HOPE	STILL	PHIFE HAND PULLING BACK CURTAIN.
77B		PHIFE	-SHOW GEAR -JACKET -HAT	BACK STAGE	-CURTAIN	BLUE BACKLIGHT	DIM	HOPE	STILL	PHIFE HAND PULLING BACK CURTAIN.
78A		PHIFE	-SHOW GEAR -JACKET -HAT	STAGE	-CURTAIN	BLUE BACKLIGHT	DIM WITH BLUE BACKLIGHT THAT FADES AWAY	DISAPPOINTM ENT/SUPRISE	JIB PULL OUT	PHIFE PULLS OPEN CURTAIN REVEALING A HAPPY FACE. HIS EXPRESSION TURNS TO SURPRISE. BLUE LIGHT FADES. CAMERA PULLS BACK REVEALS CHEERING HANDS.

SHOT #	VISUAL REFERENCE	CHARACTERS	WARDROAB	SETS	OBJECTS	FX	LIGHTING	TONE	CAMERA	NOTES
78B	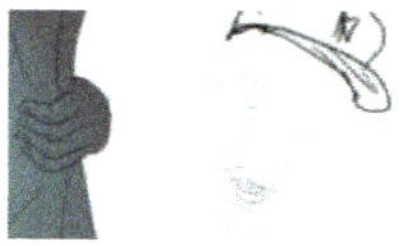	-PHIFE -CROWD	-SHOW GEAR -JACKET -HAT	STAGE	-CURTAIN -MIC	BLUE BACKLIGHT	DIM WITH BLUE BACKLIGHT THAT FADES AWAY	DISAPPOINTM ENT/SURPRISE	JIB PULL OUT	PHIFE PULLS OPEN CURTAIN REVEALING A HAPPY FACE. HIS EXPRESSION TURNS TO SURPRISE. BLUE LIGHT FADES. CAMERA PULLS BACK REVEALS CHEERING HANDS.
78C	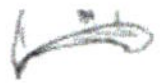	-PHIFE -CROWD	-SHOW GEAR -JACKET -HAT	STAGE	-CURTAIN -MIC	BLUE BACKLIGHT	DIM WITH BLUE BACKLIGHT THAT FADES AWAY	DISAPPOINTM ENT/SURPRISE	JIB PULL OUT	PHIFE PULLS OPEN CURTAIN REVEALING A HAPPY FACE. HIS EXPRESSION TURNS TO SURPRISE. BLUE LIGHT FADES. CAMERA PULLS BACK REVEALS CHEERING HANDS.
78D	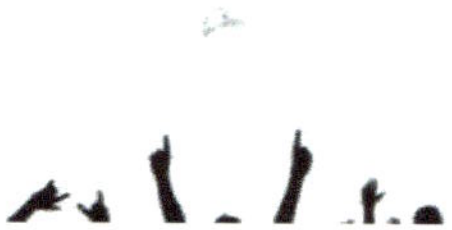	-PHIFE -CROWD	-SHOW GEAR -JACKET -HAT	STAGE	-CURTAIN -MIC	BLUE BACKLIGHT	DIM WITH BLUE BACKLIGHT THAT FADES AWAY	DISAPPOINTM ENT/SURPRISE	JIB PULL OUT	PHIFE PULLS OPEN CURTAIN REVEALING A HAPPY FACE. HIS EXPRESSION TURNS TO SURPRISE. BLUE LIGHT FADES. CAMERA PULLS BACK REVEALS CHEERING HANDS.
78E	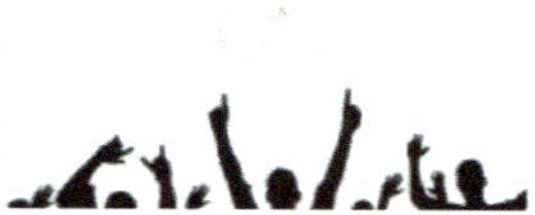	-PHIFE -CROWD	-SHOW GEAR -HAT	STAGE	-CURTAIN -MIC	BLUE BACKLIGHT	DIM WITH BLUE BACKLIGHT THAT FADES AWAY	DISAPPOINTM ENT/SURPRISE	JIB PULL OUT	PHIFE PULLS OPEN CURTAIN REVEALING A HAPPY FACE. HIS EXPRESSION TURNS TO SURPRISE. BLUE LIGHT FADES. CAMERA PULLS BACK REVEALS CHEERING HANDS.
81A	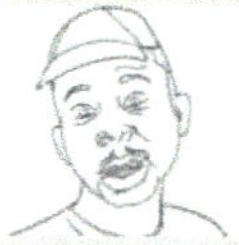	-PHIFE -RASTA ROOT	-SHOW GEAR -JACKET -HAT	STAGE	-TURN TABLES -MIC	X	STAGE LIGHTING	AWE	PAN FROM PHIFE TO RASTA	PHIFE IN AWE OF CROWD.

SHOT #	VISUAL REFERENCE	CHARACTERS	WARDROAB	SETS	OBJECTS	FX	LIGHTING	TONE	CAMERA	NOTES
81B		-PHIFE -RASTA ROOT	-SHOW GEAR -JACKET -HAT	STAGE	-TURN TABLES -MIC	X	STAGE LIGHTING	AWE	PAN FROM PHIFE TO RASTA	TURNS HEAD AFTER HEARING RASTA SCRATCHING.
81C		-PHIFE -RASTA ROOT	-SHOW GEAR -JACKET -HAT	STAGE	-TURN TABLES -MIC	X	STAGE LIGHTING	AWE	PAN FROM PHIFE TO RASTA	PHIFE WATCHES RASTA SCRATCH
81D		-PHIFE -RASTA ROOT	-SHOW GEAR -JACKET -HAT	STAGE	-TURN TABLES -MIC	X	STAGE LIGHTING	AWE	PAN FROM PHIFE TO RASTA	PHIFE WATCHES RASTA SCRATCH
82A		-PHIFE -RASTA ROOT	-SHOW GEAR -JACKET -HAT	STAGE	-TURN TABLES -MIC	X	STAGE LIGHTING	AWE	TILT FROM RASTA FACE TO TABLES	PHIFE WATCHES RASTA SCRATCH
82B		-PHIFE -RASTA ROOT	-SHOW GEAR -JACKET -HAT	STAGE	-TURN TABLES -MIC	X	STAGE LIGHTING	AWE	TILT FROM RASTA FACE TO TABLES	PHIFE WATCHES RASTA SCRATCH
82C		-PHIFE -RASTA ROOT	-SHOW GEAR -JACKET -HAT	STAGE	-TURN TABLES -MIC	X	STAGE LIGHTING	AWE	TILT FROM RASTA FACE TO TABLES	PHIFE WATCHES RASTA SCRATCH

SHOT #	VISUAL REFERENCE	CHARACTERS	WARDROAB	SETS	OBJECTS	FX	LIGHTING	TONE	CAMERA	NOTES
83A		-PHIFE -RASTA ROOT	-SHOW GEAR -JACKET -HAT	STAGE	-TURN TABLES -MIC	X	STAGE LIGHTING	AWE	JIB PULL OUT	RASTA SCRATCH CAMERA PULL OUT TO SHOW PHIFE IN FRONT OF HIM ON STAGE
83B		-PHIFE -RASTA ROOT	-SHOW GEAR -JACKET -HAT	STAGE	-TURN TABLES -MIC	X	STAGE LIGHTING	AWE	MEDIUM. JIB PULL OUT.	RASTA SCRATCH CAMERA PULL OUT TO SHOW PHIFE IN FRONT OF HIM ON STAGE
83C		-PHIFE -RASTA ROOT	-SHOW GEAR -JACKET -HAT	STAGE	-TURN TABLES -MIC	X	STAGE LIGHTING	AWE	JIB PULL OUT	RASTA SCRATCH CAMERA PULL OUT TO SHOW PHIFE IN FRONT OF HIM ON STAGE
83D		-PHIFE -RASTA ROOT	-SHOW GEAR -JACKET -HAT	STAGE	-TURN TABLES -MIC	X	STAGE LIGHTING	AWE	JIB PULL OUT. MEDIUM.	RASTA SCRATCH CAMERA PULL OUT TO SHOW PHIFE IN FRONT OF HIM ON STAGE
84		PHIFE	-SHOW GEAR -JACKET -HAT	STAGE	MIC	X	STAGE LIGHTING	APPRECIATIO N/RESPECT	STILL. MEDIUM- CLOSE	PHIFE LOOKS UP TO ACKNOWLEDGE MA DUKES PERFORMANCE: "MA DUKES"
86		PHIFE	-SHOW GEAR -JACKET -HAT	STAGE	MIC	X	STAGE LIGHTING	APPRECIATIO N/RESPECT	STILL. MEDIUM- CLOSE	PHIFE TURNS TO ACKNOWLEDGE V RICH. PERFORMANCE: "V RICH ON THE KEYS"

SHOT #	VISUAL REFERENCE	CHARACTERS	WARDROAB	SETS	OBJECTS	FX	LIGHTING	TONE	CAMERA	NOTES
90A		-PHIFE -RASTA ROOT - V RICH -CROWD	-SHOW GEAR -HAT -ATCQ SHIRT	STAGE	-TURN TABLES -MIC -KEYBOARD	X	DARK ACCEPT ONLY WHITE STAGE LIGHTING ON PHIFE	LOVE	JIB PULL IN	CAMERA SHOWS ENTIRE STAGE. FLYS OVER CROWD.
90B		-PHIFE -RASTA ROOT - V RICH -CROWD	-SHOW GEAR -HAT -ATCQ SHIRT	STAGE	-TURN TABLES -MIC -KEYBOARD	X	DARK ACCEPT ONLY WHITE STAGE LIGHTING ON PHIFE	LOVE	JIB PULL IN	CAMERA SHOWS ENTIRE STAGE. FLYS OVER CROWD.
90C		-PHIFE -RASTA ROOT - V RICH -CROWD	-SHOW GEAR -HAT -ATCQ SHIRT	STAGE	-TURN TABLES -MIC -KEYBOARD	X	DARK ACCEPT ONLY WHITE STAGE LIGHTING ON PHIFE	LOVE	JIB PULL IN	CAMERA SHOWS ENTIRE STAGE. FLYS OVER CROWD.
90D		-PHIFE -RASTA ROOT - V RICH -CROWD	-SHOW GEAR -HAT -ATCQ SHIRT	STAGE	-TURN TABLES -MIC -KEYBOARD	TRANSITION TO LOGO	DARK ACCEPT ONLY WHITE STAGE LIGHTING ON PHIFE	LOVE	JIB PULL IN	GOES INTO "A TRIBE CALLED QUEST" LOGO ON PHIFE'S SHIRT AND TRANSITIONS TO BLACK SCREEN WITH LOGO ALONE
90E		-PHIFE -RASTA ROOT - V RICH -CROWD	X	LOGO	LOGO	LOGO	LOGO	LOVE	LOGO	LOGO GRAFFIC TO BLACK

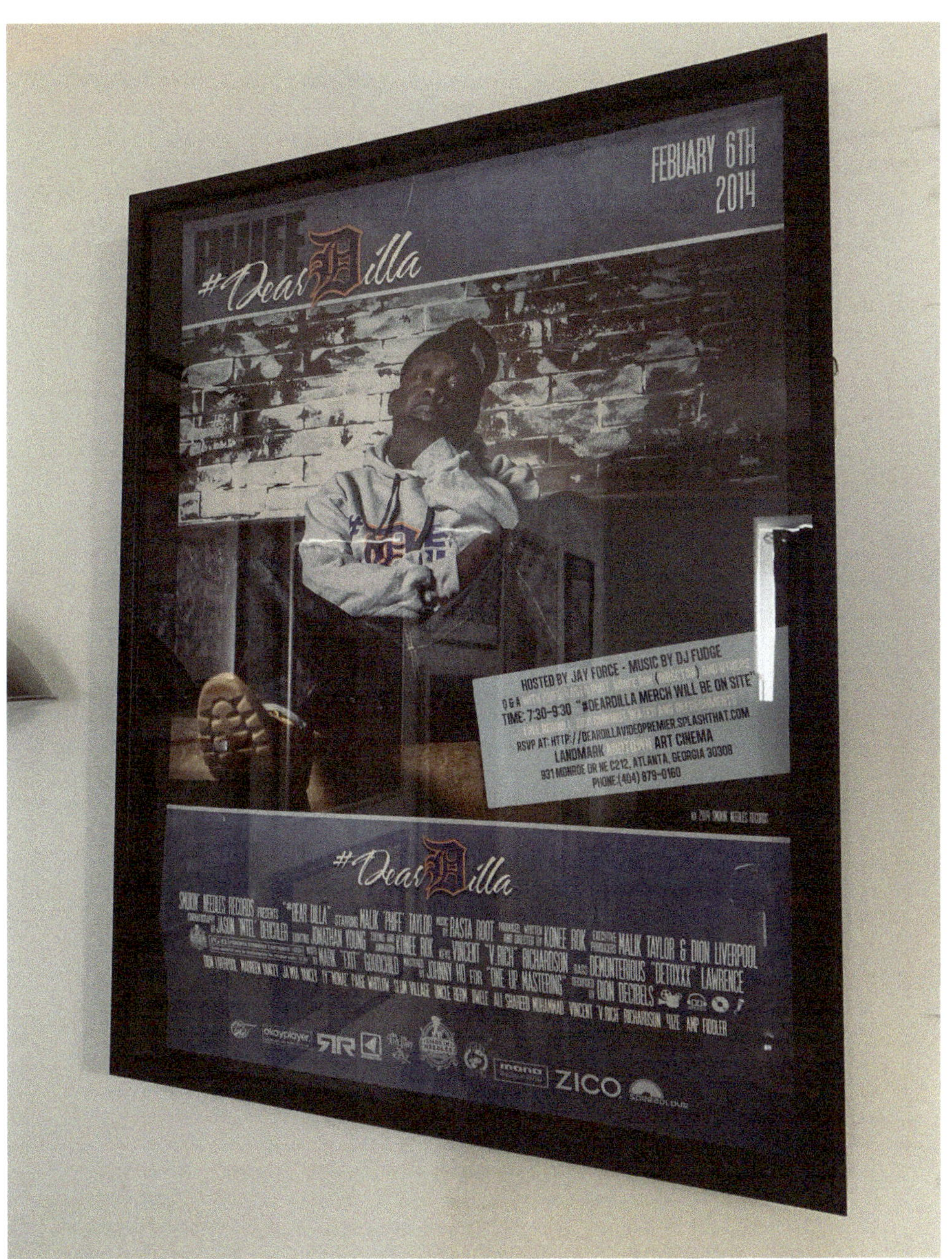
FEBUARY 6TH
2014
#DearDilla
HOSTED BY JAY FORCE - MUSIC BY DJ FUDGE
Q & A
TIME: 7:30-9:30 "#DEARDILLA MERCH WILL BE ON SITE"
RSVP AT: HTTP://DEARDILLAVIDEOPREMIER.SPLASHTHAT.COM
LANDMARK ART CINEMA
931 MONROE DR NE C212, ATLANTA, GEORGIA 30308
PHONE:(404) 879-0160
#DearDilla
"#DEAR DILLA" STARRING MALIK "PHIFE" TAYLOR
RASTA ROOT
JASON "INTEL" DECHLER
JONATHAN YOUNG
KONEE ROK
VINCENT "V.RICH" RICHARDSON
MALIK TAYLOR & DION LIVERPOOL
MARK "EXIT" GOODCHILD
JOHNNY HO FOR "ONE UP MASTERING"
DEMONTERIOUS "DETOXXX" LAWRENCE
DION DECIBELS
okayplayer
ZICO

BONUS: THE MAKING OF THE BEAT.

DJ Rasta Root, Producer: I knew that because of his production style and the level of his production, anybody doing an homage to him or a tribute, that that beat had to be really knocking. It had to be almost like he did it. But the crazy thing about the song is that there's a whole 'nother side to it. It wasn't supposed to be any of that. What happened with that particular song that I sampled from which was 'Hold Tight' by Slum Village which features Q-Tip. It starts with the drum sample. The drums come in and it was difficult for me to beat match it. The timing of it and how many bars before Tip says "Hold tight. This is the last time you hear me." So I was like, "You know what? Let me just do an edit. That's the Commodores' drums from the Slum record. Let me get the drums and add my little samples in there like the guitar riff." Because I had the "Baby" a cappella from the song he had called 'Baby' with Guilty Simpson & Madlib. That a cappella wasn't available but one of my friends did some computer trick and ended up coming up with an acapella for it. I was able to get ahold of those ad libs. Like "Let's go" and all. I was like "Let me sprinkle those in there." So all it was was the drums (the drum beat), the guitar lick, and and every once in a while he'd be saying something.

The hook part is a "Jaydee, flip another beat for me." Originally, it was saying it over and over again. It was very redundant. My friend said, "Why don't you put different beats in between it and juggle them?" Finally, I took songs he produced and just put them in the hook. "Jaydee, flip another beat for me," and I play "Climax." "Jaydee, flip another beat for me," and I play the "The Look of Love." That's how the hook was born.

So we were at soundcheck in Salt Lake City doing a show. I played it during soundcheck and Phife was like 'Yo what's that?' I said "Just something I'm working on as a little segue for me to mix an extra song in." Then he's like, "We have to do something with that." He said "Send it to me." So I emailed it to him. We have a guy named V. Rich [Vincent Richardson], who has done a lot of music for us. Phife said to him "Hey, can you do, like, an intro to the beat, and then I'll just rap over the beat itself?' The guy misunderstood what Phife said and did the piano intro you hear at the beginning of the song. Then, he ended up playing a lot of other stuff over it like a bass line and keys. He sent it to Phife and Phife was like, "Yo, I didn't ask for this, but this is incredible." But it wasn't tracked out. The bass notes were not tracked out. I had to talk to him and say "Can you send me just the stems of that and I'll rearrange it?" It took me from like 9 months from inception to completion. Just trying to get it right. Not even the goal of representing Dilla but more so because it was so intricate. We had the beat. We had the keys. He was writing the lyrics. We recorded in California. I said to him, "Imagine you're talking to your friend. He's here for a second and you're talking to him. And that's how it sounds when you hear all his ad libs in the back. It's like he's having a conversation with you or cheering you on. Or answering some of your questions."

We were listening to it, and I was, like, missing something. I talked to a bass player [Demonterious "DETOXXX" Lawrence] and said "You think it needs some bass?" He was like, "Yeah." He plays the electric bass and laid the bass over it. I said, "Embellish some of the parts. Make it beautiful" And he did that, and it kind of completed the beat. Then, I laid down the scratch bridges. I took all the samples. I cut the shit out of it and that was it.

www.ingramcontent.com/pod-product-compliance
Ingram Content Group UK Ltd.
Pitfield, Milton Keynes, MK11 3LW, UK
UKHW062313290726
14090UKWH00018B/1037